Saturday Night,
Sunday Morning

Saturday Night, Sunday Morning

SINGLES AND THE CHURCH

Nicholas B. Christoff

HARPER & ROW, PUBLISHERS, San Francisco
Cambridge, Hagerstown, Philadelphia, New York,
London, Mexico City, São Paulo, Sydney

1817

To Norman J. Ackerberg,
a friend and a source of inspiration

The text of this book is printed on 100% recycled paper.

SATURDAY NIGHT, SUNDAY MORNING: *Singles and the Church*. Copyright © 1978 by Nicholas B. Christoff. All rights reserved. Printed in the United States of America. No part of this book may be used or reproduced in any manner whatsoever without written permission except in the case of brief quotations embodied in critical articles and reviews. For information address Harper & Row, Publishers, Inc., 10 East 53rd Street, New York, N.Y. 10022. Published simultaneously in Canada by Fitzhenry & Whiteside Limited, Toronto.

First Harper & Row paperback edition published in 1981.

Designed by Jim Mennick

Library of Congress Cataloging in Publication Data

Christoff, Nicholas B
    SATURDAY NIGHT, SUNDAY MORNING.

    1. Church work with single people.   2. Single people — Religious life.
I. Title
BV 4437.C48   261.8′3   77-7841
ISBN 0-06-061381-5

80 81 82 83 84 10 9 8 7 6 5 4 3 2 1

Contents

Foreword

by Martin E. Marty, *The University of Chicago*

"Here am I, send me, send me!"

That's the spirit.

That's the spirit Isaiah (6:8) finally caught in his temple vision. It's the spirit that in the olden, golden days of missionaries the Christians used to sing about. It's the spirit that sent people to Greenland's icy mountains, India's coral strand, and Afric's sunny fountains. So they said or sang. It's the spirit that today's ministers profess when they take vows of service, and it's the spirit today's congregations 'fess up to when asked to justify their existence.

"Here am I, send me, send me!"

People are still sent, and they go. They smuggle Bibles into the Soviet Union and duck bullets in Uganda. Agents of Jesus Christ endure prisons in Korea and Chile and the hazards of America's inner cities and even its suburbs. There will be chaplains in combat zones and communicable disease wards or reconcilers in the no man's lands of divorce courts and political conflict.

"Here am I, send me, send me!"

Silence. There are zones, or at least there is a zone, that few are prepared to enter. Maybe they find the language of the old missionary hymns quaint and corny, but few of them will deny the biblical impulse behind lines like: "Loud and long the Master calleth . . ." The calling is not the problem for the church; the answering is.

Nicholas B. Christoff, one of the few "sent" and gone, reports back from behind the curtain that shields the nation's singles from their church and calls others to the hazards of the combat zone that inspires him in this book about the unmarried—even the word stigmatizes by describing people in reference to what they are not. Let me risk a wager with many of you who pick up *Saturday Night, Sunday Morning.* If you are married and either sharing life or leadership in a Christian cell dominated by the married, you will read these pages and think something along these lines: "Christoff is wrong. We care as much about singles as he does. I even secretly envy the kind of ministry he has found. True, not everything in his world is as glamorous as the media and the advertisers purport. But even the problems and the terrors he faces are more interesting than are ours—diapers, drudges, boring marriages, conventional families. Of course, if circumstances were right, I'd go into such a ministry as a member of this congregation—or its pastor. Here I'd be, I'd go, I'd go."

Then why don't we go? Christoff compellingly and tellingly shows that most of us do not. Honest preachers would wince if it suddenly dawned on them that "Pastor Nic" is sitting out there listening to the ways they talk about the nuclear family as the norm. Not a few pray-ers would like to repeal their prayers after they hear Nic report about the typical one he heard. One Sunday God was asked to "look down with *pity* upon the destitute, the homeless, *the single,* and the widowed . . ." Most could genuinely say that they wished more singles were present, or that they were better served by the families who make up the majorities or that they would kick in some dollars to support venturers like Christoff in exceptional ministries. We, willing to justify ourselves, can even point to some outstanding moments and missions that the author might have overlooked. Still, little happens.

While statistics about the size of the singles minority were familiar, I must confess that they never leaped off the page so arrow-straight to the heart as they did when *Saturday Night, Sunday Morning* pointed out that for every married couple in America there is a single adult. That's a more dramatic way of saying that one-third of the nation's adults are not married. The church of today is ready to specialize. Given time, money, and ingenuity it can find a way to comprehend and serve distinctive minorities with special needs. Somewhere there is probably a ministry for deaf, retarded, and left-handed heirs of Swiss World War I veterans in America. Christians know how to zero in with *the* mission to *the* Jew" better than they can find every third Gentile. What's wrong?

Christoff must know that the church includes millions of widows and widowers in its care, that significant numbers of divorced people are not dropped from the rolls, that not a few people who did not choose to be single but are and many more who choose to be single and are make their way into sorts of welcomes as strays in family-minded parishes. What he is setting out to do is not to overlook those now present but to look over those yet absent and to ask why. His is a radical task, one that asks the church to reconceive the way life is to be lived—its styles, forms, and intentions; its models, norms, and goals. Until church people do so successfully, they will never serve the growing and already largest minority group in the nation. If they do, funds will follow, and leaders will emerge to minister.

What holds Christians back? One restraint is a proper regard for the meaning of family life. Count me among those who would not want to see familial existence further downgraded or eroded than it is. But is the nuclear family as we now experience and define it truly normative, a biblical product? I wonder. Today's nuclear family, uprooted from tradition and tribe and clan, undercut by the surrounding culture, and collapsing from within, can be defined as "two parents, two children, and a psychiatrist." The church complicates matters by loading up the family with meanings that the Bible never intended it to have. The family is a momentary eruption in the tribe, and the tribe is an element in the larger and varied "people of God." The meanings generated among the whole people and the values transmitted through the tribe have their split-second embodiment in the family—just as they can in the company of singles. The tribe and the people as a whole cannot be comprehended in any form, familial or single. It is the sense of tribe and people that has disappeared in so much of the church's concept of social life and in the lives of so many singles.

If fear of failing the family holds some Christians back, a less easily voiced concern accompanies it. Many singles have chosen or stumbled into ways of life that run counter to biblical commands and prescriptions. Won't ministry in their company cheapen Christian standards and violate God's law? To be seen enjoying such singles' company might look like *condoning*. . . . You can hear the rest of such sentences. Well, think about fifty marriages of people who are at home in the church and are well served by it. You know what they are like and what goes on in them; they acquire their virtue from the single technical fact that their foundation "goes by the book." For the rest, isn't the act of enjoying such married peoples' company something that might look like *condoning* . . .?

Christoff is a good identifier and empathist but a very poor condoner. He even goes to the trouble of setting forth new or variant seven deadly sins in the singles' world. (Why did he have to mess up that strong chapter by finding some virtues there too!) While he can scourge the church-as-it-is, his book is written more out of hurt than of anger, of hope than of scorn. While the style is narrative in its simplest forms and the tone is often cool, a note of urgency persists.

The singles' minority is not going away. While many divorces are followed by remarriage, there are now so many divorces that the single sector almost inevitably will grow. In the state of California, not only the most populous but the pioneer, more people between the ages of twenty-one and thirty now live together as singles than in marriage. Inflation is killing the single-family home and leading builders to construct abodes for modes of dwelling that by their style almost induce the world of singles to grow. I may not, I do not, like those facts, but do I have the choice of turning my back on the people who are agents or victims of those changes? Christoff's "no" answer might well inspire countless Christians to reconceive the ordering of life and, even more, their ministry in it. His book is for singles as well as for the dwindling majority that is trying to make sense of them. Maybe we should think of his ministry in this book as a response by one single toward the zone of the marrieds who responded: "Here am I, send me, send me!"

Preface

One Sunday morning as I sat in church singing the hymns and listening to the sermon, a strange feeling came over me. I felt vaguely uncomfortable, out of place, as though I didn't "belong." This was a particularly strange feeling for a pastor, and so I asked myself, Why now and never before?

At the seminary, I'd spent most of my time writing sermons, attending classes, and guest preaching. I'd been too involved and busy with the Lord's work and the life of the church to feel out of place. The same was true of my early career as a pastor serving two different congregations. I was too thoroughly caught up with my role as leader and counselor to imagine how I might have felt in any other role.

It wasn't until after I'd accepted a new assignment to serve not another church but a chain of apartment complexes where approximately four thousand singles lived that I began to see myself as a bachelor as well.

So there I was in church, stripped of my role as a leader—no Bible class to teach, no windows to open, no candles to light, no sermons to deliver. For the first time in my life, I became acutely aware of my single state as I sat there without a wife and children at my side. The hymns were good, the choir so-so, but the sermon seemed to come from another galaxy. It wasn't even remotely related to my world, my needs, my frustrations, and my aspirations as a bachelor parishioner. Looking over the congregation, I saw children, teen-agers, members of the youth choir, and parents scattered throughout the church, but I saw nobody else who might have felt excluded, as I did, by a sermon that made a hero of the husband and father.

Why did I feel as though I had been slapped? Why were there no singles in those pews with whom to discuss my feelings of resentment and inadequacy?

Why do so few singles, for whom Saturday night looms as the bright, tantalizing promise, show up in church on Sunday morning?

I began my search for these answers that very Sunday, in June 1973. This book, five years later, is the result of my research and full-time ministry with single people in the United States.

Acknowledgments

Many people have contributed to the creation of this book.

First and foremost is Carole Ashkinaze who suggested the title. Her clarifying organizational skill and editing expertise were of immeasurable value.

Dr. Elmer N. Witt's research and insights about clergy and Dr. James Davis's research and survey of church attendance have provided strength and depth.

The friendship of and numerous conversations with authors Jerry Gillies, for his skill and insight in human growth and development; Hy Steirman, for his wisdom and advice; and Sue Lindsay Roll, for her skill, insight, and ear for a quote, have been extremely helpful.

Reverend Donald D. Johnson, Mary Johnson, Dr. William D. Streng, and my brother Ted have provided continual insight, wisdom, support, and encouragement.

Paul E. Gallagher, Carolyn Myss, Martha Hopkins, Peggy Schmidt, Patrick Remy, Mary E. Langer, Larry McIntyre, Tom Lovell, Marty Tabis, Pat Lavelle, Julie Davis, David Handley, and Martin E. Marty have graciously in one way or another given time and opinions.

And to the thousands of singles throughout the country who consented to offer an interview, an opinion, a statement, I owe my gratitude. In some cases I have used fictitious names and locations for persons mentioned in this book so that their privacy will be preserved.

1. Singles: America's Largest Minority

A new and, in many ways, privileged group of people has arrived on the American scene. This group encompasses more diversity of opinion, life-style, and background than any other population bloc in America. I'm talking about the unmarried, the separated, the divorced, and the widowed, the single parent as well as the swinging bachelor, the unhappy "late bloomer" as well as the angry loner. Together they constitute America's largest, most significant, and least understood minority—the single men and women in our society. And suddenly they are too numerous and too outspoken to be ignored.

One out of three adult Americans is single. For each married couple in our land, there is a single man or woman. Unexpectedly, they total over forty-eight million, double the number of Americans who were single a scant twelve years ago.

More than half of them are over thirty and can remember when the single state was almost universally considered an aberration, an affliction, a shame, for which the only known cure was "get married."

Once upon a time, the term *single* was generally understood to refer to those unmarried and under thirty. For the over-thirties there were other, more pejorative labels: spinster, hermit, recluse, queer.

Not any more. One-fourth of all singles are over sixty-five. Twelve million are widows or widowers. The smallest group of singles—the divorced—turns out to be the most rapidly growing group of all. For the first time in American history, singles under thirty comprise a *minority* within the vast single population as a whole, and to continue to regard all singles as members of an afflicted, amorphous group is to deny them the dignity they have a right to expect as human beings.

Singles deplore the stereotypes with which they are depicted in advertisements, in the press, and by their married "friends." Their lives are *not* jampacked with racquetball, ski trips, swimming parties, and exciting jobs. Their nights are not occupied with an endless round of parties, bar-hopping, and bed-hopping. The stereotype of the singles scene as a hedonist's nirvana is deplorable to singles, many of whom lack the money, the "Pepsi generation" good looks, or the time to indulge in the swinging life-styles attributed to them. As one tall, pot-bellied Chicagoan in his thirties told me, "If I had done half the stuff people think I do, I'd probably be dead by now." Another bachelor in his late twenties, who'd tried to live up to the stereotype and had fallen short, admitted, "I've been to practically all the bars, and I can tell you this: It's not so easy to score."

Can you *imagine* forty-eight million single Americans on a never-ending quest to quench their insatiable sexual thirsts? It makes exciting copy, and it does sell everything from magazines and newspapers to toothpaste, cigars, and health club memberships. But if it's a true characterization of the way they live, why aren't the churches clamoring to enfold them? And if it's false, why do the churches, with self-serving and exclusionary sermons, shut out the few devout singles who turn up on Sunday?

The married majority tends to look upon the singles scene with a mixture of envy and pity, at once jealous of the Madison Avenue stereotype and sorry for the "poor souls" who have been unable to find a marriage partner and live the wholesome American Dream. It must be a lonely life, filled with depression and grief over one's inability to adjust, the marrieds reason. It's a triumph of faulty logic by which marrieds are able to rationalize their own commitments and shun the temptation to break free.

The truth of the matter, as unmarried Chicago hairstylist Carole Breust puts it, is, "We work, just like anybody else. You have to work hard to be able to afford to live these days, and I really get tired of reading all these articles about how much fun I'm having."

But thanks to the feminist movement, with its emphasis on the dignity of the individual, and a plethora of consciousness-raising books and programs ranging from Transactional Analysis groups to Gestalt and primal therapy workshops, the single person is now being encouraged to pursue career, hopes, and dreams with a sense of quiet pride. We're living in what author Tom Wolfe has dubbed the "Me" decade; personal awareness and self-acceptance are the goals.

Most people, historically, have *not* lived their lives as if thinking, "I have only one life to live." Instead they have lived as if they are living their ancestors' lives and their offspring's lives and perhaps their neighbors' lives as well. They have seen themselves as inseparable from the great tide of chromosomes of which they are created and which they pass on. The mere fact that you were only going to be here a short time and would be dead soon enough did not give you the license to try to climb out of the stream and change the natural order of things . . .

And now, many dare it! . . . They did something only aristocrats (and intellectuals and artists) were supposed to do—they discovered and started doting on *Me!* They've created the greatest age of individualism in American history! All rules are broken! The prophets are out of business! . . . the great religious waves have a momentum all their own. Neither arguments nor policies nor acts of the legislature have been any match for them in the past. And this one has the mightiest, holiest roll of all, the beat that goes . . . *Me* . . . *Me* . . . *Me* . . . *Me*. . . .[1]

As more and more singles discover that they need not be bound

[1]Tom Wolfe, "The 'Me' Decade and the Third Great Awakening," *New York* 9, no. 34 (August 23, 1976): 40.

by scripts of the past, that they need not hang their heads in shame for opting to remain single, that they have the capacity to carve out meaningful lives for themselves in which they can be useful—and even inspiring—to others, that they are OK, the failure of established churches to accept them on those terms is bewildering. Why isn't the church at the forefront of the consciousness-raising movement? they ask confusedly. Why isn't the church encouraging them to realize their fullest human potential? Why doesn't the church allow them to maximize their God-given talents and skills to their own benefit and the benefit of others? Why does the church insist, "Get married"?

Born singly into the world and destined to die singly, unmarried men and women are beginning to glow with a newfound pride in their ability to *live* singly. It's won them respect, even admiration, in the marketplace.

Builders, food and furniture manufacturers, legislators, and resort owners all court them with studio or one-bedroom apartments in luxury developments, with space-saving furniture, single-portion frozen dinners, tax-reform bills, and low-cost singles' weekends. The business world has discovered that singles have more disposable income—a mind-boggling $205 billion a year—to spend on entertainment and luxury items. Their married sisters and brothers are tying up earnings in mortgage payments, life insurance and retirement funds, second cars, and nest eggs for the kids' college educations, redoing the kitchen and adding a family room, and as a cushion against inflation.

Singles make up the largest concentrated pool of sales prospects in the country today. More than half of all Porsche sports cars sold in 1974 were purchased by singles. Forty percent of the Americans who buy Gremlin subcompacts are singles. In metropolitan areas, half of all Visa card holders are unmarried.

What's more, an appeal to the singles market is good for business generally. An ad depicting a well-dressed young man surrounded by admiring females can persuade a happily married man to purchase a suit of clothes geared to the bachelor's life-style. The singles' preference can spell the success or failure of entire lines of products from booze to automobiles and clothing. Whatever your business, the most successful entrepreneurs have learned, just run an ad depicting young, carefree, sexy, vibrant-looking men and women enjoying your product, and you've tapped a fresh source of endless spending. It took appeals from feminist groups and publications and a nationwide campaign for "truth in advertising" to persuade advertisers to cast women in their thirties, as well as sexy, young girls of eighteen and nineteen, in television commercials for laundry detergents, floor wax, and squeezable paper towels.

Why? Because the singles scene looks like fun. And quite often, it is. At least for the few who are not too homely, too old, too frail, too fat, too skinny, too strapped with financial problems, too insecure, too plagued by acne, crooked teeth, or myopia, and too far removed—by the demands of their jobs, schools, geography, or their own discomfiture with an "endless summer" in a world beset by poverty, injustice, and disease—to fit precisely into the carefree, glossy, technicolor world of ads and movies.

But what of the many—the elderly, widowed, divorced, or less-well-endowed singles—for whom life is not an endless, acquisitive, materialistic joyride?

Doesn't the church realize it was young singles who marched on the Pentagon during the first massive demonstration against the Vietnam War? Doesn't it realize that young single people—none of them swinging jet-setters on a lark—were murdered at Kent State in the '60s and in vast numbers in Southeast Asia well into the '70s? Doesn't the church realize that single men and women laugh and cry, triumph and fail, love and grieve, stray and seek answers and a sense of purpose and direction just like the rest of us?

Doesn't it care?

2. Sunday Morning: Where Are the Singles?

The proprietor of a popular New York singles bar describes his establishment, with its Tiffany lampshades, piped-in rock music, and three-dollar hamburgers, as a place where "predatory men prey upon neurotic women and where impotent men are preyed upon by castrating females." His place fills a social vacuum, he believes, adding, "Let's face it. People don't meet at church anymore."

Looking out across the sea of faces at a typical Sunday morning service can be a reassuring or frustrating experience for a pastor, depending on his or her vantage point. What does one see? Families. Two and three generations of them. And often, in the faces of the youngest, one can see a kind of rapture. Young minds being touched by new and exciting concepts—how they fit into the divine scheme of things, ways to enrich their own lives. There is a strong sense of communality in the Bible readings, prayers, and songs. Surrounded as they are by those who love them—parents, grandparents, and children—it is easy to feel the love of God. Surely, this is a reassuring observation for any pastor.

But, wait. Where is Ed Jones, whose wife is filing for divorce? And the Darcy twins, who are attending college right here in town? What about old Mrs. Fogarty, who never missed a Sunday while her husband was alive? And where, oh, where are all those Sunday school graduates who must be in their twenties, thirties, and forties by now? Moved to another town, perhaps? Are they attending church *anywhere?*

Where *are* the single men and women, young and old, never-married, oft-divorced, or bereaved, who, according to the latest census figures, make up fully one-third of the average American community? Why aren't they *here* where they "belong" on Sunday morning?

To hear singles—encountered at poolside, at singles bars, in bus stations, in counseling sessions, anywhere but church—tell it, church is the last place where they can experience a sense of "belonging." They are condemned by their pastors for engaging in premarital sex; yet they live in a society that is strongly influenced by Helen Gurley Brown's *Sex and the Single Girl,* by *Playboy, Playgirl,* and *Penthouse* magazines, by *Deep Throat,* by the pill, and by the widespread availability of legal abortions. In other words, society seemingly condones what the church condemns. Singles are ignored in sermons extolling the nuclear family and are often denied the opportunity to marry out of their denominations. They feel cheated and shut out by the rigid, unbending church. Some couples living together in what the established church roundly denounces as a state of "sin" instinctively know themselves to be involved in more loving, committed relationships than the marriages of their own parents. They are turned off by what they see as the hypocrisy and dishonesty of the church itself.

Nor are these couples ignorant of the life and teachings of Jesus. Didn't he plead for compassion on behalf of the prostitute, Mary Magdalene, urging "him that is without sin, cast the first stone"?

"If Jesus were the pastor in our church," offers a twenty-nine-year-old Californian who has been living with his twenty-six-year-old girlfriend for the past six months, "I'd be in the front row every Sunday. I'd feel I had as much right to be there as anyone else. I wouldn't be afraid to discuss my questions about sexuality and God with him.

"But sometimes I feel I know more about 'Christianity' than the guy up there in the pulpit. There's no forgiveness, no compassion, no humility in *him*."

He and his girlfriend believe they are "good" Christians in line with the teachings and spirit of Christ himself. They are kind to children and animals, honor their mothers and fathers, spend three evenings and a Saturday afternoon each week doing volunteer work for a local antipoverty agency, shudder at the thought of inflicting physical or emotional pain upon another human being, and are tolerant of those who hold views different from their own. Her father is a heavy drinker who slaps her mother around when he's had a few too many. But the young couple are teetotalers and health food addicts who believe in keeping their bodies healthy and clean out of respect for themselves and each other. And yet, in the eyes of the church, they are "sinners," unworthy to receive communion and the blessings of the heavenly Father.

The church, by cleaving steadfastly to the ideal nuclear family as symbolic of the ultimate good, denies communality—in fact and in spirit—to those not wed. And so the unwed seldom go to church, which in itself is a failure in the eyes of the preacher and congregation since for the church establishment the bench mark is Sunday morning.

The singles aren't there; "proof" in itself, many clergymen declare, of the way they are being "corrupted" by society. It's a rare preacher, priest, or rabbi who stops to ask whether he or she might be contributing to the alienation of singles by the tone and content of his or her own sermons.

Where *are* the singles on Sunday morning?

The answer is disarmingly simple. Almost any place where they can experience a sense of peace and contentment on their "day of rest" in a nonthreatening environment, where they can "fit in" without having to endure the hostile stares or uncomprehending sermons of those to whom their unmarried state is an aberration and a threat, wherever they are welcomed with open arms and without reservations or, at least, left in peace.

The California couple (mentioned above) like to drive out to a wooded glen on Sunday mornings. There, with a picnic basket and a Bible they feel "closer to God." They take turns reading to each other, pausing here and there to discuss the import of a passage.

Others seek the companionship of peers at urban singles bars that serve Bloody Mary and Eggs Benedict breakfasts, or they play backgammon, bridge, or tennis in the clubhouses, or on the courts of their own apartment complexes or at the beach. In the company of other singles who work hard and play hard the rest of the week, they receive more support than from their pastors and elders in church on Sunday. Some give in to physical exhaustion, sleeping till noon on Sundays, and rationalize their behavior with an eye on Genesis and Exodus. "To rest on the seventh day—that's a biblical injunction isn't it?" asks Norman, a Chicago athlete. "And where is it written that the only service of the day must be held at 9:15 A.M.? If they *[the clergy]* really gave a damn about people like me, they would schedule another service at noon or even at eleven o'clock. The schedule of services at my church—and everything else that goes on there—is geared to accommodate people who are in bed by 10 P.M. on Saturday night. Married people. Families."

And then, Sunday morning finds some singles in somebody else's bed. "How on earth," asks Brenda, a thirty-eight-year-old, unmarried Atlanta secretary, "can a girl who is sinning in the eyes of the church participate wholeheartedly in a religious experience when everything in it is geared to make her feel shame for what happened last night?" Brenda is not promiscuous but has sat through "sermons that made me feel like a whore," she says. Except at Christmas and Easter, she hasn't been to church for more than six years.

The New York singles bar proprietor was correct in asserting that singles don't form friendships in church any more. To find one another, they must look elsewhere. To learn the reasons for their staying away, one must approach them on their own turf— in bars, apartment complexes, and pool clubs where they feel secure.

The Bar Scene

The singles-bar scene is the same, whether at a pub in Davenport, Iowa, or at a discotheque on the Sunset Strip in Los Angeles. There are peanut shells on the floor at one, velvet and chandeliers at the other. Accents and sophistication vary with the geography, but the clientele is drawn from the vast population of the divorced and unmarried in search of the same things—companionship, a way to pass the time in a relaxed setting, and an end to the loneliness that comes from feeling unloved.

Sunday through Thursday nights are slow periods in most bars that cater to singles; these places come into their own on Friday nights, when unattached men and women stroll in—singly or with friends of their own sex—in hopes of landing a Saturday-night date. They continue to swing through Saturday night when many singles come back to dance to live rock bands or to escape the monotony of Carol Burnett and "Saturday Night Live" on TV. Most of these bars swing into Sunday morning when they serve gourmet brunches at reasonable prices to singles to whom the thought of eating breakfast alone is depressing or who hope to get the jump on next Saturday night by lining up a date ahead of time.

Great quantities of liquor are consumed, cigarettes smoked, and fingernails chewed in what, for many, is a terrifying, nerve-wracking process. As Cindy, a twenty-three-year-old clerk-typist confided over a glass of white wine at T. G. I. Friday's in New York, "I hate this place. I hate having to wait in line to get in.

I hate being pushed around by mobs inside. I hate the way the guys look you up and down when you walk in as if you were a piece of meat. I hate the guys who look you in the eye five minutes after meeting you and ask, 'Your place or mine?' I hate the ones who don't even bother to make a pass but just walk through the place, handing out their phone number to girls they assume are hard enough up to call them. But I come here every Friday night. I force myself. When you've spent the rest of the week in an office where the only male is old enough to be your grandfather, this is the only hope you have of meeting datable men.

Cindy was promptly admonished by her friend Susan, a twenty-two-year-old stewardess who thrives on the bar scene. "Just relax and enjoy yourself, for Pete's sake. You're never going to catch anybody's eye with that pessimistic attitude and that hangdog expression on your face." Susan was having a ball. "I love to dance. When I am dancing, I can forget about preparations for emergency landings and the old goats hounding you for a deck of cards, a copy of *Newsweek,* or another cocktail when you're trying to get out a meal service," she explained. "There may not be any special guy in my life right now, but I can always find someone to dance with in a place like this. And, you know, you don't *have* to go home with anybody if you don't want to."

Susan, a Methodist from Nashville who moved to Manhattan three years ago, was surprised to be asked about church in this setting. She does attend Sunday services on her infrequent trips home—three or four times a year—but rarely goes to church in New York. "I like to go to church with momma and daddy and my little brothers; I'm at home in that church. But the last time I went to church up here, a chill went right through me. I introduced myself to the pastor on my way out, and you know what he said to me? He said, 'All alone in the big city, are you? You ought to find yourself a husband.'"

"I've had it with my church," said Douglas, a real estate broker in his late twenties. We sat over bacon and eggs at the

Colorado Mining Company, a popular singles hangout in Atlanta. It was Sunday morning. "I've listened to sermons about the joys of motherhood, about the blessedness of the holy state of matrimony, bringing up the kids to know Jesus, and the evils of booze and 'illicit sex' until it's coming out my ears. And not just at one church. I shopped around, trying six or seven. I can usually find a friend to tell my troubles to in a place like *this,* but those churches don't give a hoot about the problems that single people have."

"Church is for families," declares an Atlanta woman, who hasn't had a family of her own since her husband left her for someone much younger six years ago. "Our lives used to center around the church, but a long series of experiences has taught me that you don't fit in as you did when you were married. My biggest disappointment was in discovering that in none of the three churches I attended following my separation and divorce was there any provision made for single folks. We are perhaps the loneliest people in the world, and it just seems better to worship in solitude and not upset the smug, confident, happily married clique."

"I'd really like to be married," says Malcolm, a San Francisco stockbroker who is still nursing the wounds left by the departure over a year ago of his girlfriend of three years. "I was really in love with that girl. She wore my ring for six months and gave it back when some tycoon from New York began sending her roses and expensive jewelry." Malcolm functions pretty well during the week when the demands of his job leave him scant opportunity to indulge in self-pity. But when Saturday night rolls around and he can't muster up the courage to ask another girl out, he feels the knife-edge of loneliness and despair.

"And church on Sunday has become absolutely unbearable. Just to see all those married people, smiling, singing out, holding one another's hands, with their children at their sides, is painful enough, but those sermons make me feel like a total failure in the game of life. I'm not living the good Christian life with a good Christian wife and kids, and I stick out like a sore thumb."

"Let me ask you something," offers Harry, a thirty-five-year-old, twice-divorced insurance salesman who works on a commission-only basis. He isn't earning enough to pay the rent and is being sued by his first wife for back alimony and child support payments. "If you couldn't even take care of *yourself* and went to church to pray for guidance because you had nowhere else to turn and your ex-wife was doing her darndest to turn the kids against you, how would *you* like to listen to a sermon about the joys of wedded bliss?" Harry sat, drowning his sorrows in a cut-rate happy hour beer at a Chicago singles bar on a Friday night. "I'll probably be right here on this same barstool come Sunday morning if I can put together the price of a Bloody Mary," he added morosely.

The bar is a place where singles can, if they choose, submerge their identity and the problems gnawing at them in the laughter, the music, the tinkling of ice in glasses, and the camaraderie of strangers—without jeopardy to their professional standing or self-respect.

For many, the singles bar even performs a function that was once thought to be within the exclusive purview of the church and family life. "I find that a night with old friends, or spent making new ones, is a tremendously regenerative type of experience," says Bart, a Washington, D. C., bachelor engineer. "It recharges my batteries for the week ahead."

THE SINGLES APARTMENT COMPLEX

Sam Matthews left his wife one cold November night in 1974 and, having no place else to go, persuaded a divorced colleague to let him "camp out" on the sofa of his Chicago apartment until he could find a place of his own. Within hours of his arrival, he found himself longing to be back in the seven-room suburban house with its gingham kitchen curtains, his three children snug and asleep in bed upstairs, "Home Sweet Home" on the walls, and a wife to take care of him. But with the marriage irrevocably and bitterly ended, he couldn't go back. So he settled for an apartment in the sprawling International Village singles complex in suburban Schaumburg.

Location was an important factor, Matthews said over coffee in his sparsely furnished but efficiently appointed bachelor quarters. It's close to his job at O'Hare Airport, and it's a short twenty-minute ride to his children on visiting days. Even more important, no children are there to trigger painful memories of happier days.

"I didn't want to be reminded of my family, and I wanted to be where people understood the situation; so a singles complex seemed the right choice," explains Matthews, who, like many others, was unable to find much compassion among the married neighbors he'd left behind. "I liken it to a tire factory, a retread factory, where people whose emotions are worn out can come to be retreaded. It takes some of us longer than others, but they move out when they are ready to face the real world again. It's a safe haven in which to find friends, get your confidence and security back. I think we have to grow up again once we come here, and when we do, we're ready to face the world again."

A similar sentiment is expressed by Mack, who moved into the sprawling Riverbend singles complex in Atlanta following his divorce. He lived there three and one-half years before remarrying and buying a home. "At Riverbend," says Mack, who'd lived in a sparsely furnished Alpharetta, Georgia, subdivision house with his first wife for eleven years, "I had neighbors I could talk to. Exchange recipes with. Borrow a couple of tablespoons of coffee from. That sort of thing. It seems trivial, but it was terribly important to me at that stage of my life to be able to have some kind of human contact. My wife's friends and neighbors froze me out whenever I ran into them, especially in church."

People live at singles complexes for a variety of reasons. Some, like Matthews and Mack, view it as a sort of sanctuary. To some younger residents, it's their first home away from the home where they grew up. In the words of one twenty-two-year-old International Village resident, "A singles complex represents a newfound freedom, like taking off your girdle." Some see the singles complex as a logical extension of college fraternity or dormitory life; it's a life-style that fits their personal needs as they get started on their careers. Others see it as a temporary dwelling in which to live while shopping for that hard-to-find brownstone with wood-burning fireplace, within walking distance of their inner-city jobs. For some singles, it's an opportunity to meet members of the opposite sex. As Mary Louise, a thirty-year-old employee in the traffic department of a Chicago television station observes, "Don't knock it unless you've tried it. I'm kind of shy, and I feel a lot more comfortable about striking up a conversation with the good-looking guy down the hall than with a good-looking stranger in a bar about whom I know nothing." And finally, some wonder what all the fuss is about. They view their apartments as just a place to live, without the hassles of home ownership, whether in the proximity of other singles or not.

Some apartment developers openly advertise their complexes as "singles communities" or "adult communities" to promote an image of their apartments as a "fun" place to live. Others deplore the image, believing it detracts from the "respectability" of an apartment community, particularly a luxury community catering to older residents who don't want to be kept awake by stereos turned up full blast in adjoining apartments.

An apartment builder was dismayed when his suburban Chicago development, Four Lakes, began to acquire a reputation among young, unmarried apartment-seekers as a singles complex. Designed to take advantage of its natural surroundings instead of bulldozing them into history, Four Lakes offered lush landscaping, wood-burning fireplaces, four lakes (stocked with bass, sunfish, bullheads, and carp), and ample facilities for tennis, swimming, skiing, sailing, biking, and archery. Singles began to move in, in large numbers, to take advantage of these amenities. But their loud parties, sometimes bordering on rowdiness, have tended to drive off some prospective tenants, who happen to be married.

On the other hand, the developer of a downtown Chicago complex recently went so far as to name his community the Satyr and to promote it in sales brochures as a haven "for lovers and livers . . . Hedonists, and SHEdonists" in search of "all the physical pleasures. Anything goes!" In the opinion of a number of Chicago singles, such brazen publicity went beyond the normal levels of taste and propriety.

"The assumption is that if you're not committed to a marriage you must be on a great quest for sex every night. This appeals to people's sexual insecurities," complains a young, female, Chicago-based advertising consultant. "And that only serves to perpetuate the sexist stereotypes I've been fighting as a feminist and the discrimination I've encountered as a single." She lives in a singles complex a short distance from the Satyr, she told me, "and it's no den of iniquity, I can assure you."

Giana Lane, rental manager of the International Village singles complex in Schaumburg, Illinois, remarks, "When people learn that I work here, I invariably get the same reaction—you know, the ho, ho, ho, *that* place, the sex bin. They picture constant partying and boozing, girls running naked in the hallways, fornication on the stairs, that sort of thing. It infuriates me because I've been in the other world. I spent fourteen years in that little suburban neighborhood with its white picket fences, and I would venture to say that there is more hanky-panky going on in that little suburban neighborhood—I mean overt wife-swapping and the whole bit—than there is here."

And yet, singles complexes are often seen as beyond the pale, outside the reach of a neighborhood church. In most U. S. cities, from the major metropolitan areas to the smallest towns, new homeowners are constantly receiving invitations—sometimes printed, sometimes extended in person by the pastor or a member of the ladies' auxiliary—to attend nearby church services. A frequent pitch is to "consider making our congregation your church home." Apartment dwellers rarely receive such solicitous attention.

"I practically had to beat down the pastor's door to get somebody to talk to me about getting on their mailing list and getting copies of the church calendar," complains a Decatur, Georgia, engaged woman. She plans to share her new apartment with her husband once they are married and until they can afford to look for something larger. "What are we, some kind of freaks? Just because we don't live in a house yet? Just because we're single?"

"The rabbi greeted me warmly," comments a Long Island, New York, unmarried graduate student who had expressed interest in affiliating with a Jewish congregation a few miles from the college campus. "But the finance committee chairman, to whom he referred me, didn't make me feel very welcome. He wanted a one-hundred-dollar annual membership fee. This was a discounted rate for single members and seemed reasonable. But he also asked me to sign a pledge to contribute five thousand dollars over the next three years to the temple's building fund. I barely earn enough, working nights and summer vacations, to cover my tuition. Those were his terms, and I was forced to reject them." "I was told I needn't join the synagogue to come to sabbath services whenever I like," observes an Atlanta, Georgia, writer who was raised as a Jew. "And why not? I've been to Friday-night and Saturday-morning services at the synagogue in my neighborhood, and the *shul* is always empty. But you can't be admitted on high holy days if you're not a member, and the fees are pretty stiff. I hate to admit it, but I've just sort of let the whole thing go."

"My neighbors thought I was crazy when I moved in and began

asking about churches in the area," says a Denver resident. I spoke with him one Sunday morning while he was waiting for a tennis court to become vacant at his luxury southwest singles complex. "They told me that the residents of our complex were discouraged from joining, but I refused to believe them. I went alone and found out what they were talking about. It wasn't anything so blatant as 'we don't want you here.' It was subtle: wary looks from members of the congregation, a mother who called to her children—who'd been headed for the row where I was sitting all by myself—to follow her to another, more crowded pew a few rows back.

"A wife and some kids of my own would have made me respectable enough for them, I think," he adds. "But what kind of Christians are they anyway if you have to be married to feel a part of their prayer services?"

CONSCIOUSNESS-RAISING GROUPS

Jack wasn't likely to be found in church *or* in the singles scene comprised by the discothèques, pubs, and apartment complexes of Chicago. Since the breakup of his marriage, he'd divided most of his time between the office where he works as an accountant and the suburban house in which he rents a small, basement apartment. At thirty-three, he saw the worlds of Saturday night and Sunday morning as equally remote. Laurie had divorced him. His work was slipping. He didn't like himself.

I might never have known of Jack's existence if he hadn't walked into my office one rainy April afternoon. He was confused, lonely, and worried. After several weeks of struggling with himself, he'd finally admitted he couldn't solve his problems alone. He needed help.

Jack is one of the nearly six million divorced people in this country who make up a growing percentage of the single population. He's one of those we've come to recognize as the "walking wounded."

No matter how civilized the divorce, it's a rare spouse who can emerge unscathed by the pain of separation. A marriage reduced to a lot of legal complications, tying you up in court for months or even years, is one of the most traumatic experiences any man or woman can go through. There's almost always an undercurrent of failure, even in an era when one out of every three marriages ends in divorce.

"What happened to the look of love in his eyes when I told him we were going to have a baby?" "What happened to that feeling of closeness we had in that summer cottage at the lake when just a touch said all there was to say?" "How did I fail her?" "Why does he resent me?" "How could it have ended in such ugliness and indifference?"

Amid the arguments, the self-incriminations, and the degradation of the courtroom, many divorcing partners find it difficult even to remember that they shared good times. The question is, Where do they go from here?

"I'd been raised to think there really was a Pepsodent family—a mother, a father, and 2.5 children who never slobbered when they brushed their teeth—you know?" muses Valerie, a Chicago photographer. Valerie is one of a growing number of women who've decided that they want something more than whiter-than-white washes and creative casseroles, but many neighborhood churches and fellow parishioners do not consider such desires "healthy" or "normal."

The courts, the large number of state legislatures that have rushed to ratify the Equal Rights Amendment, and an increasing number of employers and creditors have come, with Valerie, to the realization that she need not be satisfied with a whiter-than-white wash, that she has a right to aspire to "something more."

The church, on the other hand, stands apart, one of the last bastions of male chauvinism. "I've never felt rejection so keenly as

I did in the church I've been going to all these years, after I left Harry," says Valerie. "Harry didn't blame me for the failure of our marriage, but our pastor did. It got so I would walk the other way when I saw him headed in my direction with that pitying look on his face. That's why I joined a therapy group. I know I need help, but I'm not going to get the support I need in church."

Betty, Megan, and Ron have never been married, and at the ages of forty, thirty-two, and forty-one, respectively, they have begun to wonder if there's indeed "something wrong" with them. This, and the fact that they sought help in a Chicago Transactional Analysis group, are the only ways in which they are linked. They lead widely divergent lives—Betty is a hardworking copywriter, Megan is an independently wealthy supermarket heiress whose days are devoted to fund-raising activities and volunteer work at a children's hospital, and Ron is a college professor who dates several women and for the most part enjoys his bachelor existence.

It's Betty's co-workers, Megan's parents, and Ron's married friends who got them wondering how they'd "failed" to wind up happily married with the requisite number of children. Their respective churches have only fed their guilt about "failing."

"All those smug families" is a recurrent refrain in therapy sessions whenever the subject of church comes up.

"Church can't help me to feel good about who I am and where I am in my career, but I *am* learning to feel OK about myself in the company of people like Megan and Ron, really 'together' people who would just rather remain single," says Betty, "like me."

"I see my life in different phases—high school, college, law school. Now I'm trying to establish myself in a profession. I don't have the time or energy to tie myself to a woman," offers Craig, a young lawyer from Chicago who has been involved in a similar group for the past two months. "I wouldn't be giving a wife a fair shake. That's why I'm single at this point."

"Being single," says Kirk, a Chicago engineer, "enables me to put four thousand dollars into a grand piano. I'm not sure a wife would put up with a grand piano in a one-bedroom apartment. I wouldn't have been able to spend money this way if I were married. But I hate to have to keep defending my decision to remain single."

Lawrence, a homosexual, joined a Chicago consciousness-raising group. He has sustained what he calls a "supportive, loving relationship" with his male roommate for more than four years. His parents, his boss, and his co-workers have no idea that he's gay, however, and Lawrence, a personable, exceptionally good-looking, and athletic blond, is tormented by the fear that he might be "found out." "I don't want to change. I'm not capable of changing. This is the way I am and I'm comfortable with it," he declares. "But my mother would have a heart attack if she suspected. I work for a very strait-laced company, and they'd get rid of me so fast it would make your socks fall down. I need help in dealing with people who won't leave well enough alone, advice on how to refuse courteously their matchmaking efforts and how to justify the fact that I'm still not married. I'll be thirty-six in May, and the pressure to accept a blind date is overwhelming. But can you imagine what kind of reception I'd get if I confided in the Lutheran minister down the street?"

For still other troubled singles, pressures of the church itself can be a source of problems warranting therapy.

"I believe in God, but I don't go to church anymore," declares a twenty-five-year-old Chicago schoolteacher who was raised a Catholic. "My church drove me crazy. All that incense and pomp and circumstance. And last Easter, this new, young priest started yelling about people who hadn't come to church every day during Holy Week. I haven't been back, and I don't know if I ever will. I can't take church like that."

Unbending rules and regulations have also turned an unmarried, fifty-five-year-old dental assistant away from her Catholic upbringing. "As a young woman, I used to be very much into my religion, but I didn't believe in confession," she admits in the course of a therapy session. "I just didn't feel I could go in and confess to another human being because he really didn't know what was in my head and my heart. You could say whatever you wanted, and he would grant you absolution. Then you could go out and commit the same 'sin' all over again. I felt that God would know what I was really sorry for, regardless of what I said to this man in the confessional. So I stopped going."

It took a lot of courage for those two women to talk candidly about their religious views. Despite a long disaffection with the church, they had emerged with an almost equally damaging burden of guilt for having left.

What they needed most desperately, and what they sought in one of the group therapy workshops becoming increasingly available in American metropolitan areas, was support, respect, and acceptance for *what* they are—and not merely *in spite* of what they aren't—from other people. The void created by the absence of the church in their lives cried out to be counterbalanced with some means of sustaining their faith in God and in their fellow human beings. The void created in the lives of these and other "walking wounded" is, sad to say, rarely filled within the confines of the unbending establishment church.

LIVING TOGETHER

Despite the injunctions of established churches and synagogues, young adults are becoming increasingly interested in alternatives to traditional marriage—group marriage, trial marriage, contract marriage, homosexual unions, collectives, communes, and even the near-celibacy dictated by the Hare Krishna sect. They've also tried living together without marriage, saying in some cases that their relationships are stronger for it; in others, that the "illicit" union carries no fewer risks and no less pain upon separation than does holy matrimony.

"When it comes down to the nitty-gritty and you actually

divvy up the lamps, the dog, and living-room rug, it's no less a hassle than divorce," says a Chicagoan whose live-in arrangement fell apart last year.

"On the other hand," he adds, "there weren't any children to fight over and to carry the emotional scars of our failure to make it work."

Despite the fact that the church calls it a "sin," he admits he would try it again before rushing into a marriage that might have an even more tragic dissolution.

Morality aside, living together makes sense to an increasing number of young adults and even to a good many widows and widowers past their prime and unwilling to sacrifice their individual Social Security benefits for a legal and sanctified union. Hermione and Marty, a Miami couple in their late sixties, decided that by pooling their resources they could move out of the dreary, government-subsidized senior citizens project in which they'd met and into a small apartment within walking distance of the beach and golf course where they liked to while away the sunny afternoons. But marriage, in their case, would have meant a loss in their combined incomes of $110 a month. "It was either live apart or live in sin," chuckles Hermione with a twinkle in her eye. "Marty's rabbi was outraged when he told him about our plans, but I have found this lovely man with whom to spend my golden years, and I don't really give a hang what anybody thinks of us."

Many younger couples are living together openly, with the full knowledge and tolerance—if not enthusiasm—of their parents. Barbara Hirsch has written an excellent book about the legal ramifications of living together; and there have been countless magazine articles on the "etiquette" of living together, including pointers on how to break the news to the folks, how to introduce one another at social gatherings ("my man," "my woman," "my friend," and "my lambcake" are among the suggestions in one such guide), and how to choose among the wide variety of contraceptives currently available.

Marilyn lived with Larry for about six months before they

married. She is among the thousands to declare, "I'm glad we lived together. It helped us understand each other's needs. I knew what he liked, and I think our premarital experience put our marriage on an exceptionally solid foundation."

As for Larry, "I doubt if I could have been persuaded to get married any other way. I was scared of marriage for a long, long time. Most of my friends had married six or seven years earlier, and most of them aren't with their original wives. That's unfortunate, not only for them, but for their children. I was afraid marriage would not only wreck our relationship but would put all kinds of pressures on me to stick with it, come hell or high water." What Larry found out, in his six-month-long living arrangement with Marilyn, is that "there's more comfort in learning to share good times, money problems, whatever comes along, than in having to go it alone."

Some of the most vocal advocates of living together are divorced singles who are almost unanimous in their hindsight that living together before marriage could have made all the difference. In Paula's case, a serious sexual incompatibility surfaced after her marriage to Bob and contributed greatly to the breakup. "If only we'd lived together first," she sighs. "I never even thought about it at the time. It was a moral no-no. But I would never, ever get married again without living with someone first. Never."

For some couples, young and old, living together is beginning to look like a sensible alternative to rushing headlong into marriage. But in the eyes of the unbending church, it's still a "moral no-no." That's why the only "sanctuary" many such couples know is the privacy of their own houses and apartments.

SENIOR SINGLES

Senior singles grumble and complain less than anyone else about the church. "My children were all baptized and married there. I was married there. We had my husband's funeral service there. I love my church. I have many fine memories of church," says Anna Jacobsen, an eighty-one-year-old widow who lives at the Lutheran Home and Services for the Aged in Arlington Heights, Illinois. "Of course, I'm not well enough to go to Sunday services any more. But my pastor came to visit me on my birthday last year."

But Margaret Eliza Kuhn, the seventy-two-year-old founder of the Gray Panther movement, considers "arrogance of our condition, a sin," as she put it in her keynote speech to a 1975 gathering of health specialists and social services administrators in Chicago. "Our liberation cannot be seen in isolation in a just and humane society. . . . One of our slogans is get them off their asses and into the classes."

While the church is aware of senior singles, much more needs to be done to combat their sense of abandonment—by their church as well as by their secular families.

"Isn't it awful?" asks the elderly resident of a Chicago retirement home. "I spent all my life raising five children, caring for them, nursing them when they were ill, and now not one of them wants to take care of me."

Elderly singles wish the churches would "stop writing us off, before we're even in the grave," as Elsa Morgan, a recently bereaved widow in Phoenix, put it in a letter to me. The chartering by some churches of specially equipped buses that will accommodate wheelchairs to transport residents of senior citizens homes to Christmas and Easter services and special church functions is one innovation Mrs. Morgan would like to see extended to parishes throughout the nation. Senior citizens who begin to feel desperately out of touch after infirmities prevent them from attending services on a regular basis also would be grateful for newsletters to keep them abreast of church and parish life.

In 1970, one out of ten persons in the United States was sixty-five and over, a total of 20.1 million men and women, which includes married persons. Of that total, 1.5 million older persons lived alone or with nonrelatives; one out of four, on incomes of less than 1500 dollars a year, or 29 dollars a week.[2]

"What our residents really need," says Paul Hower, executive secretary of the Lutheran Home and Services for the Aged, "is a sense of dignity, accomplishment, and a reason to get up in the morning."

Wherever they are, whatever their life-styles, the greatest problem encountered by single people at every age level and in all walks of life is the depression caused by loneliness. The fear of loneliness itself is enough to drive hundreds of thousands who loathe the singles scene into bars and apartment complexes that cater to others like them. The reality of loneliness can be a genuinely debilitating experience, leading to pathological depression, for which professional counseling may be required.

Most of us are able to combat occasional loneliness by seeking the support and solace of others, particularly in the church setting. But the single adult—unmarried, divorced, or widowed—all too frequently is stopped by a brick wall of intolerance from taking refuge in the established church and is forced to look elsewhere, singles say.

"Alone" time can be contemplative time, discovery time, creative time, inner growth time; but many parishes, looking askance at the congregant who marches to a different drummer, exact a stiff price of whoever would join them: conformity. For those unable or unwilling to be remolded, the penalty is rejection.

Discrimination is another serious problem for those who stand apart from the nuclear family, the norm in our society. They pay higher taxes and insurance premiums than married people; they have to search harder for apartments because many landlords

[2] U. S. Department of Health, Education and Welfare, Office of Human Development, Administration on Aging, *New Facts About Older Americans*, June 1973.

prefer "stable, married" tenants; and they are bypassed for promotions and job offers because they are considered transient and undependable.

Under the Tax Reform Act of 1969, singles pay as much as 20 percent more in taxes than married persons with identical incomes. Still, things have improved since Vivian Kellums waged her campaign in 1948 to change tax laws that required singles to pay as much as 41 percent higher taxes. And the fight goes on. Singles have learned that there is strength in numbers, and organizations like CO$T (Committee of Single Taxpayers) continue to press for additional reforms.

Single women tend to have more problems obtaining credit and mortgages. The National Census Bureau Report on Marital Status indicates that on the average a never-married male executive with a college degree makes a yearly income just barely equal to the income of a married executive with a high-school diploma.

Singles get the short end of the stick in the game of life itself. Actuarial tables indicate that singles don't live as long as married people and that the single man's hospital stay is nine days longer than a married man's, presumably because there is no one at home to care for him during convalescence. As if this weren't enough, research comparing the levels of happiness between married and single men and women give the wedded the edge. In a study of twenty-three-year-old men and women, single and married, at the Mental Research Institute at Berkeley, California, scientists found that the single man ranks highest in signs of severe neurotic symptoms.

The established churches are not totally without concern for the single men and women in adjacent communities; many pastors claim they would dearly love to see the singles return to the fold if only they knew how to go about it. But so far, say the alienated men and women I talked with in the course of my research, many churches' efforts to deal effectively with the triple-edged sword of loneliness, discrimination, and rejection have been laughable. To try to attack these problems by setting aside an evening and a room for a monthly singles group is like trying to solve the problems of the aged by building more old folks' homes. "It's a sop," says a Lutheran schoolteacher who attended one such event at her church on Long Island, "to get us out of their hair."

To put a singles night on the calendar is effectively to wash one's hands of any other responsibility for what many clergy as well as lay church leaders persist in viewing as a "misguided, afflicted" group. No wonder attendance at these functions is so poor. Or haven't the church fathers noticed?

Few singles are in church when the announcement is made, and few are on the parish mailing list. Who then can reasonably be expected to attend such functions? A bachelor who is hounded mercilessly by his church-going parents to find a "nice Christian girl and settle down" so they can "die in peace"? A woman driven by family pressures to find a mate before she is past child-bearing age?

It's not entirely impossible that a pair of desperate, frustrated, resentful people will meet and find happiness together, but Moira, a chic Boston travel agent, is highly skeptical. "I consider it extremely unlikely that two insecure, unhappy people will know how to make each other happy," she says. "And a secure single can find a way out of the singles maze without depending on the church to find him or her a mate."

Some attempts by the Catholic church and the leading Protestant denominations to "modernize" and "update" Christianity seem equally ridiculous to author Tom Wolfe.

. . . the Catholics gave the nuns outfits that made them look like World War II Wacs. The Protestants set up "beatnik coffeehouses" in church basements for poetry reading and bongo playing. They had the preacher put on a turtleneck sweater and sing "Joe Hill" and "Frankie and Johnny" during the hootenanny at the Sunday vespers. Both the priests and the preachers carried placards in civil rights marches, gay rights marches, women's rights marches, prisoners' rights marches, bondage lovers' rights marches, or any other marches, so long as they might appear hip to the urban young people.

In fact, all these strenuous gestures merely made the churches look like rather awkward and senile groupies of secular movements. The . . . Urban Young . . . found the Hip Churchman to be an embarrassment, if they noticed him at all.[3]

Wolfe believes that the most "rational, intellectual, secularized, modernized, updated, relevant religions—all the brave, forward-looking Ethical Culture, Unitarian and Swedenborgian movements of only yesterday" are, ironically enough, on their last legs.

Believe it or not, theorizes Wolfe, what the urban young people want from religion "is a little *Hallelujah!* . . . and *talking in tongues!* . . . *Praise God!* Precisely that!" He points out, correctly, that in the most prestigious divinity schools today it is "charismatic Christianity" that can be found in the forefront of the new avant-garde movement. The election by a clear majority of Americans of a Southern Baptist president, who spoke candidly, throughout his campaign of being a "born-again Christian" with a "personal relationship" with Jesus, is noteworthy in this regard.

"We don't want our churches to be mating services," complains Moira, the travel agent. "We don't want them to lead protest marches, and they don't have to pick up guitars and sing secular songs to get us interested in God. We're believers, most of us, and what we ask of the church is *religion.* All we ask is that they allow us to participate in the religious experience without trying to change us. Can't they give us sermons that will excite us and inspire us, married and single, without putting us down? Is it too much to expect a little Christian charity and love from the church itself?"

[3] Tom Wolfe, p. 35.

3. Saturday Night:
Where Is the Church?

Single Christians who look for the sustenance of friendship in their churches frequently find instead a stone of frustration. Some "single young adults" groups pile party upon party, but conversation—if it ever gets started—rarely goes anywhere. Other groups slip into Sunday evening sermonettes that have scant significance for Monday morning —or Saturday night.[4]

"You can never find a taxicab or a minister when you really need one," an unmarried Chicago schoolteacher complained to me in a wry attempt at humor.

Where is the church on Friday afternoon when a single man who's just been laid off could use a sympathetic ear and some practical advice? More often than not, the parish phone is answered by a secretary or, even worse, by an answering device.

"Rev. Fletcher is not in. If you will leave your name and a number where you can be reached. . . ."

But if only there were someone to talk with right now!

To make matters worse, calls from singles who are infrequent attendants and seldom tithe are going to be low on the pastor's list of priorities when he returns.

[4] Editorial, "Toward Authentic Piety: Church and the Single Person," *Christianity Today* XIII, no. 19 (June 20, 1969): 23.

Singles have serious problems and only an elusive memory of the way in which Sunday school seemed to provide all the answers to the questions they had as children. If their problems and their deep yearnings for a cleansing, cathartic kind of experience can't be met by the established church, they'll look elsewhere: to the Jesus movement, the Reverend Sun Moon's Unification Church, est, transcendental meditation, Transactional Analysis, and other encounter group experiences. They will find communality as well as catharsis in such groups, and they will be welcomed without question and without disdain for their sometimes unconventional life-styles.

Where *is* the established church when a troubled single adult's world seems to be falling apart? When an important relationship or a job comes to an end? When a call to the parish office is to no avail?

What *are* its preoccupations? What vision of ministry is it which excludes one out of every three people in the United States from serious consideration in a church's scheme of things? Can it be attributed to deliberate neglect on the part of church councils and planning boards or to oversight?

"Don't we matter at all?" is the question many disaffected singles would put to church leaders if ever they were given an opportunity. And it's a fair question.

What churches *do*, they do well, decently, and in order, as the wise counsel of Holy Scripture suggests. But do they do enough?

With what are churches and their leaders preoccupied today? Preservation is a dominant concern, not only the preserving of souls, but preserving the financial well-being, property, and family-oriented status quo. To be sure, these are all valid concerns and as far as they go could not be faulted, but they serve to exclude singles, at least by omission.

Scrutiny of a typical church council meeting would evidence this oversight. First, the make-up of the meeting precludes a knowledgeable or sympathetic attitude toward the concerns of singles. The typical pastor has been married for thirty years and has several children. All church officers are married men with children, and they own their homes. Seldom are young singles or apartment dwellers represented. Those in attendance represent the status quo and the nuclear family ideal. Even the teen-age youth committee is often a placebo to reinforce the participation of the nuclear family.

PRESERVATION OF PROPERTY

Property and financial reports are usually the first order of business. The council meeting begins with reading the minutes and the treasurer's report—a detailed account of the church's financial standing at that moment, usually impressive in its scope and depth. Trends and percentages, comparing budget and income in previous years, are provided. If giving is down for the quarter, specific adjustments are suggested for meeting such financial obligations as property insurance, pastor and staff salaries, the cost of maintenance, heating and lights, telephones, printing, and so forth.

Next comes the congregation's stewardship report. How are members doing on meeting their pledge commitments? What about the building fund and debt reduction plans? If things look grim, someone is apt to suggest that a letter be written and mailed to all church members, pointing out that God loves a cheerful giver and that we shouldn't rob God of his rightful tithe. Perhaps a series of talks by prominent parishioners on the importance of giving could be appended to the Sunday service? The pattern, technique, and style of the report may vary from time to time, but not its thrust.

From the property or building-and-grounds committee, there's an elaborate report on the condition of all church property, coupled with recommendations for its efficient upkeep. Attention is focused on a sticking kitchen cabinet door which when jerked open spills bottles in a noisy cacophony of shattering glass, disturbing the Sunday school lesson in the next room; repairs are needed. The condition of the church lawn, pews, organ, altar, stained-glass windows, and cracks in the tarmac of the church parking lot are also considered in turn.

Shouldn't church officials devote time and attention to finances and property? Of course. But even at this early stage of the meeting, shortcomings of today's churchdom begin to emerge. Family men of property hold property as their first concern. If more money is needed to maintain church property, suggestions are the stagnant reflexes of like minds: the standard follow-up letters and talks to the usual, overburdened givers. Once again, apartment-dwelling singles are ignored, in a dual sense. They are not sought as officers to inject fresh techniques for fund drives, and their plentiful resources are not plumbed for additional funds.

Preservation of Status Quo

As the council meeting progresses, the omission of singles from the church's attention becomes more pronounced. Consciously or not, church officers reinforce their exclusionary concern for the nuclear family—the status quo of the congregation. From the deacons come reports on who and how many are attending Sunday morning worship services, special gatherings thought to enhance the spiritual life, such as cottage meetings, Bible study sessions, and personal house calls.

The education committee reports on its Sunday school lesson themes, its plans for teacher recruitment, the need for updated, visual teaching aids in classrooms, and the fact that the piano needs tuning. Adult education classes may be suggested, considered, approved, and scheduled. To which mission church should we donate our outdated, used, Sunday school materials?

The nominating committee presents its new slate of candidates for church office for review, evaluation, and voting by secret ballot. The "new" slate essentially renominates those sitting officers whose terms are expiring.

The evangelism committee chairman, calling for a community survey of new homeowners, expresses a sincere desire to win more souls for Christ, which would also have the desirable effect of increasing church membership. He does not mention the new, high-rise apartment complex by the shopping center.

The youth committee, represented by teen-age congregants, is given an opportunity to express its appreciation to the church fathers for their continued support and leadership. Its representative sometimes injects a request for permission to conduct a car wash on church property or to organize a cake or rummage sale to raise money for a winter retreat or national convention.

The pastor reports on new members, house visits, hospital calls, the shut-ins, confirmation instruction, ideas for a new preaching series, and denomination news. He concludes on a spiritual note of gratitude to God for having blessed the parish with such capable, talented, and dedicated leaders as those serving on the church council.

Throughout the meeting, all attention has been focused on the bulwark of status quo—the nuclear family. The pastor and deacons enumerate their personal *house* calls, and the evangelism chairman proposes a study of new *home*owners. The children of nuclear families are attended to with support for their Sunday school, car washes, and national retreats. Apartment complexes are not mentioned. And even teen-agers outrank single adults by having representation at the council meeting!

An examination of any church newsletter offers additional insights, indicating what a church is actually doing and what meetings are scheduled from week to week. Adult choir and bell choir rehearsals, confirmation classes, women's groups, Sunday school teacher conferences, Boy Scout and Girl Scout meetings, and adult education classes are standard entries, satisfying the needs of the average nuclear family.

In fact, churches serve the needs of children, teen-agers, and their parents very well!

A married woman with three children in school, for example, could find support and helpful companionship from the women's groups. Friends of like mind share medical information about what flu or vaccination shots the children should have, tips on who's who in the community and on what model station wagon can be used to transport an entire Little League team. In such groups, concerned parents find confidants who can be trusted and are pleasant to be with, who can be helpful in solving baby-sitting problems, and who can be called upon to help should an emergency arise.

This thrust is not difficult to understand in view of the fact that the average Protestant pastor has a wife, a family, and similar concerns of his own. Apt to idealize the nuclear family as God's divine plan for humanity in his Sunday sermons, he will quickly discover that he is all the more readily admired, enfolded, and accepted as the established minister in that congregation for continuing to do so.

But do his obligations end there?

What about those men and women on their own, no longer—or not yet part of—nuclear families? What about the burning social issues of our time—pollution, nuclear proliferation, over-population, and poverty? What about the jobless, hungry, oppressed, and imprisoned? Where do they fit in the parish scheme of things? What about the impacts of abortion and the pill, politics and government, international diplomacy and new tensions in the Middle East?

More than a decade ago, Dr. James H. Davis, director of the Department of Research and Survey of the National Division, Board of Missions of the United Methodist Church, suggested that some churches may have "too narrow" an idea of what a "family" actually is. His table, "Family Types in the Life Cycle," shows the attendance-participation habits of many persons as

LIFE CYCLE OF CHURCH ATTENDANCE: A SCHEMATIC REPRESENTATION

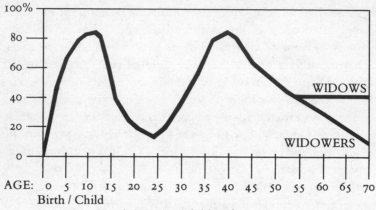

Birth / Child

Youth / Young Adulthood

Young Couples / with Children

| | Middle Couples | Older Couples | Widows Widowers |

Data compiled by Dr. James H. Davis, Research and Survey, National Division, Board of Missions of the United Methodist Church.

they progress through various stages of family life (see p. 38).

"Can we be confident that we do not seem to say to these people [singles and married couples without children] that full human potential and obligation to God can be realized only in marriage and the rearing of children?" he asked in "These Are Families, Too," an article in a church publication.[5]

Dr. Davis suggested that it is possible for those who are outside the nuclear model, or "common families," as he calls them, to "be repulsed by the church's emphasis on the Christian family." This is the case of a lonely, deeply troubled woman whose husband is

[5]James H. Davis, "These Are Families Too!" *The Methodist Story* 9, no. 2 (February 1965): 28. Material within brackets added by the author.

rarely at home. "I've been to that church since I was a little girl. They all know me," she sighed, explaining her reluctance to discuss the problem with her own pastor.

The church too often is content with serving its self-interest by idealizing the status quo—in this case, the nuclear family—as the standard for Christian living; in so doing it limits its potential by locking out Christians who don't happen to fit the pattern.

Today, more than forty-eight million adults, eighteen years and up, are outside the nuclear family circle. This total, in itself, presents a threat as well as a challenge to the traditional patterns of family and church life.

In the opinion of Dr. Elmer Witt, campus pastor at Governor's University, south of Chicago, the churches' failure to accommodate the needs of disaffected single adults is only the tip of the iceberg.

In his provocative book *Can The Church Make It?* Witt cites "disappointment, dissatisfaction, and disillusionment" as clearly identifiable trends among active churchgoers and even clergy in many parts of the country. As Dr. Witt points out, church attendance and financial contributions are down, and serious internal conflicts are emerging with regard to doctrinal differences, the need for wider societal involvement, and the newly divergent life-styles of members and their families. All these sources are of sharply increasing concern to church people.

"More destructive," he maintains, is the discernible "indifference, apathy, and disinterest" among congregants themselves. And, says Witt, it's reached "massive" proportions.[6]

"The inability of the church to act on its faith really disturbs me," says Gregg Smith of Barrington, Illinois. Gregg is the father of three and is an active member of St. Matthew Lutheran Church. He has a deep and abiding commitment to Christianity. "I wish

[6]Elmer N. Witt, *Can the Church Make It?* (Nashville: Thomas Nelson, Inc., 1972), p. 12.

Family Types in the Life Cycle			
Life Events	Family Type and Duration	Family Relationships and Responsibilities	Church Attendance
Birth	Family of Orientation, 18–24 years	The family into which a child is born teaches patterns of living. Most young people live at home until 18–24, under the influence of parents. Mostly from his family an individual learns to think of himself as a certain kind of person and adopts a set of values which he carries throughout his life.	Children attend or do not attend church school and church as parental authority dictates. More than one-half of adults surveyed follow the pattern of attendance or non-attendance set by their parents.
Independence	Single Adulthood, 1–10 years	Some single young adults live apart from families. They take upon themselves the responsibility for using their time, money, and skills. Rebellion against parents may determine some of these choices.	Single young adults make their own choices about participation in church activities. This appears to be the point at which many choose not to attend.
Marriage	Potential Family, 2–3 years	Young marrieds without children are in a transition stage. With their own families not yet established, their lives frequently appear to continue the dating phase, with late Saturday nights, sleeping Sunday mornings.	Many may postpone assuming mature responsibilities, including participation in church organization activities

Birth of Child	Conjugal Family, 20–30 years	Children change a family's way of life. The infant affects the time schedule; the older child involves the family with neighbors; the school-ager brings home demands for time and money from P.T.A., Scouts, and other groups—drawing the family toward participation.	Regular church attenders-participants rise to one in three among parents of one or two children—and to two in five for those with three or four children.
Children Leave Home	Residual Family, 10–20 years	This type has become increasingly important. The U.S. Census Bureau estimates that man and wife have about 14 years to themselves after children leave home. Many invest energy in "self-improvement" and take up hobbies and activities they have always wanted but didn't have the freedom, time or money for earlier.	They are less active in the organizational life of churches. Only one in three attends church or belongs to church organizations.
Death of Spouse	Widow or Widower, 5–10 years	Older persons increasingly tend to maintain their own residence separate from their children as members of the family are scattered. The average widow has about 16 years of widowhood before death if she does not remarry.	Half of the widows belong to some organization in church as well as being regular attenders. No widower interviewed attended church.
Death			

SOURCE: James H. Davis, "These Are Families Too!" *The Methodist Story* 9, no. 2 (February 1965): 29.

more churches would get out from behind their walls and start doing something worthwhile for people in the community. To prove out faith in God we must back up our faith with action," he insists. "I get so disgusted with the church's failure to risk and become involved with helping the poor, the needy, and those who need God's love the most." Smith's concern for people generally can be demonstrated by the organizations he helped to create: an emergency fund for needy people in Chicago and Loans and Investments for a Future Together (LIFT), a self-help organization for black businessmen in Kansas City.

Churches get so caught up with the business of building their sanctuaries, electing officers, and writing their constitutions that too often their real reasons for existing become submerged. Some churches are so polished and organized in their conduct of financial matters that they could serve as models for the business world. For example, churches often charge outsiders stiff fees to utilize church facilities for weddings and meetings. It's a cold and calculating business approach at best, rather than a love response to people in need who might be enticed into the church.

Church council members, some of whom may never achieve prominence in the business world, zealously guard their parish powers. And woe to anyone—visitor, outsider, or new member—who tries to upset the apple cart. Apathy and indifference among those who remain, and a corresponding decline in membership, are practically inevitable.

"If you can't fight 'em, join 'em. If you don't want to join 'em, stay away" is the seldom articulated but clearly perceived warning to anyone considering reform.

I am reminded of how carefully the church council of St. Mark Church in Mt. Prospect, Illinois, on which I served for two years, scrutinized a list of more than fifty female candidates for a seat on the church council in its zeal to appoint the "right" one, the one who would fit in. Such an appointment was long overdue on the historically all-male council; even so, it took an extraordinary amount of courage, determination, and persistence on the part of council president Bob Schmid to persuade the rest of the council to go along.

It took the Marble Collegiate Church in New York City until January 1977 to drop the word *male* from its standing rules regarding eligibility for the office of elder and deacon. Should a woman be found to qualify and have the desire to serve in such a capacity, she could now be considered although no such appointment is anticipated at the present time.[7]

Pastors serving Protestant churches are nearly all married. I know of one unmarried pastor on the staff of a church in Dallas, Texas, but he's the exception to the rule. It's almost impossible to find an unmarried minister serving as senior pastor of a large church anywhere in the United States. Even in churches whose members include large percentages of single people, unmarried pastors are not sought.

Frequently, formidable barriers between churches and between denominations create an atmosphere in which churches try to outdo rather than serve each other. Doubt, uncertainty, and honest questioning are seen as a threat or as evidence of a lack of faith, rather than a search for truth—and with catastrophic implications. These walls, these barriers, perpetuate what I consider a kind of "closet piety" that offers little or no promise of help, direction, guidance, or companionship to those who don't clearly "belong."

Some people on church councils, boards, and committees, who call themselves Christian, are party to very un-Christianlike behavior during the week—discrimination, bigotry, and hypocrisy. Norman Mailer goes so far as to compare "Cannibals and Christians" in his book of that title:

[7] Cf. The Marble Collegiate Church Bulletin, Reformed Church in America, Fifth Avenue and 29th Street, New York, New York, 23 January 1977, General Notices, p. 4.

What characterizes Christians is that most of them are not Christian and have no interest left in Christ. What characterizes the Cannibals is that most of them are born Christian, think of Jesus as Love, and . . . [are excited by] the thought of whippings, blood, burning crosses, burning bodies, and screams in mass graves. Whereas their counterpart, the Christians—the ones who are not Christian but whom we choose to call Christian—are utterly opposed to the destruction of human life and succeed within themselves in starting all the wars of our own time, . . . ; these Christians also succeed by their faith in science to poison the nourishment we eat and the waters of the sea, to alter the genetics of our beasts and to break the food chains of nature.[8]

When one looks deeply into the way Christian churches conduct their business in our times, one is prompted to wonder, along with a character in the Broadway musical *Oliver,* "Where, Oh, Where Is Love?"

Have we forgotten how Jesus described his life's work and purpose: to preach good news to the poor, to heal the brokenhearted, to comfort the afflicted, to give sight to the blind, strength to the weary, and liberty to the oppressed?

Have we forgotten that the ministry of Jesus was deeply concerned with the human condition? The forthright honesty of Jesus' commitment to respond to the needs of the people, at the risk of losing the establishment's support, is vital to an understanding of what he was all about. He called things the way he saw them. To the scribes and Pharisees of his day, he said:

"We played the pipes for you,
and you wouldn't dance;
We sang dirges,
and you wouldn't be mourners."

For John came, neither eating or drinking, and they say, "He is possessed." The Son of Man came, eating and drinking, and they say,

---

[8]Norman Mailer, *Cannibals and Christians* (New York: Dell Press, 1966), p. 4.

"Look, a glutton and a drunkard, a friend of tax collectors and sinners." Yet wisdom has been proved right by her actions. (Matt. 11:17–19, JB).

Concern for the human condition is a genuine and appropriate way to express deep religious feelings without being strapped to a denominational tag, without cloistering oneself. It seems to represent an honest and direct way to deal with God and encounter his divine presence.

Yet what percentage of the time allotted to conducting business by a church council or church assembly is spent dealing with the human condition?

What percentage of money is spent on community programs, the recruitment of new residents, and the needs of the poor?

One can't help but be startled and disappointed by the amount of time, money, and effort expended by mainline denominational churches in pursuit of their own, self-serving preoccupation with institutional survival.

Who benefits from the church as it is presently structured?

Is it the divorced person, a "failure" in the eyes of all too many parishioners?

Is it the single person, who is on the verge of discovering life and emerging into a fuller, more human individual yet who is in need of acceptance, direction, and encouragement from the church? Can he or she find it there?

Do the widow and widower find the support they need to cope intelligently with bereavement? Do they find a renewed sense of purpose to sustain them through their autumn years?

If they do not benefit, why not?

Who benefits from the church? The nuclear family benefits from the church. Those to whom all the family-oriented programs and activities are geared may find it difficult to understand just how uninviting an image they project to the rest. They are apt to bridle at any inference that they function more as closed corporations or social clubs with discriminating membership requirements than as Christian congregants motivated by noble intentions. Their error is in their failure to see themselves as others see them.

From the vantage point of a family man "on the inside" of the structure that serves him so well, it's almost impossible to understand why anyone would want this band of families who form the bulwark of our nation's economic and cultural stability to change its style, outlook, and emphasis. Current practices, rituals, and attitudes have been accepted for years and have served well in the past. Why knock a good thing? they demand in self-righteous indignation. Isn't it enough that in theory the church accepts every person as a child of God and claims that all are welcome?

"Anyone can come and worship God at my church," declares the hard-nosed preacher of an affluent Lutheran congregation in a small Connecticut town.

But can they really?

Singles, divorced people, and the widowed are proper subjects of concern for sermons and selections of prayers; but a pastor's excessive attention to a group outside the vocal majority who pay his or her salary can lead to a reevaluation of his or her usefulness, an investigation of motives, an inquiry into personal life, and ultimately dismissal.

While sitting in church one Sunday morning, I recall hearing the minister intone: "We pray, Heavenly Father, that you will look down with *pity* upon the destitute, the homeless, the single, and the widowed. . . ."

How would you feel if you were one of the more than forty-eight million singles in America listening to a prayer like that?

As a pastor, I enjoy visiting other churches from time to time and have found that presiding pastors seem to enjoy introducing their clerical colleagues when they happen to spot them in the crowd of regular worshipers. But as a single man, aside from my credentials on the clergy roster, I have felt isolated and excluded from the churches' inner circle of camaraderie, much like the rest of my unmarried friends.

Bishops scanning lists of seminary prospects available for positions or pastorates within the church system tend to overlook the few candidates who have been so unwise as to have failed to find suitable spouses before graduation. Some bishops personally couldn't care less about marital status but wisely realize that their constituent parishes may not be so tolerant.

Questions are raised. Why *isn't* she married? Is he gay? Can't he get along with women? Can't she get along with men? How *does* he achieve sexual fulfillment? How will she cope with "our" problems—as husbands, wives, parents, and children—unless she has experienced the highly desirable state of wedded bliss?

In the Greek Orthodox and Roman Catholic denominations, a priest cannot ascend to the rank of bishop unless he *is* single, but Protestants like their leaders to reflect their fondest self-images.

Singles, even unmarried clergy, are frequently made to feel unwelcome in the church "family"; the all-too-prevalent stereotypical notions about the way singles live feeds the fires of intolerance and prejudice among them.

What factors are behind the ever-widening gap alienating singles from the church establishment? I put the question to a variety of churchmen—lay leaders, church council members, clergymen, and ordinary, churchgoing family people.

Most put the blame on the singles, asserting that unmarried, divorced, or widowed people, but most particularly that single young adults:

- Operate on a time and interest schedule that's different from that of families.
- Are unstable, transient, and uncommitted and therefore cannot be dealt with on a long-term basis.
- Are turned off by a pitch to discipline.

- Have only themselves to blame if they feel "unwelcome" in a church family made up overwhelmingly of parents and children.
- Have so many diversions when they're young that they prefer to "put God off" until they have spouses and children of their own.
- Don't realize their need for a Savior, which is "their problem, not ours." .
- Aren't there (particularly on Sunday mornings) to be served.
- Would have more power if they weren't in the minority.
- Are at fault if the presence of Jesus in the lives of churchgoers isn't "enough for them."
- Have no right to an apology for the churches' failure to "cater to" them.

Others put the blame on the secular leadership, the mostly married congregants and church council members, declaring that:

- Married men occupy the seats on church boards and councils and run them to suit their own, family-oriented needs.
- Church members are self-centered, wanting everyone to conform to their life-styles.
- "Different" life-styles and ideas are a threat to the homogeneous majority, who are marriage- and family-minded.
- Married women want to "protect" their husbands from those "available" single women.
- Parents only attend for the sake of their children. Why should the childless and unmarried be expected to think any differently?
- Members don't do enough to make the singles feel welcome when they do come to church; members are usually too busy greeting and talking with their own, married friends.
- The vast majority of social activities and programs are geared to the married and to those financially able to participate.

• Church councils feel that activities *ought* to be geared for the majority who, after all, participate the most.

A smaller but not insignificant number place the blame squarely on the shoulders of the pastor and religious staff or their superiors. They feel that:

• The clergy consider it the church's duty "to reflect the family-oriented society" in which it is located.
• Clergymen feel personally threatened by life-styles that don't conform to the "nuclear family" model on which the stability of their congregations is founded.
• Churches have failed to use modern, up-to-date "sales" techniques to sell religion to those who may be out of touch.
• They put too little emphasis on faith and too much stress on conformity.
• The educational programs within their sphere of influence are geared more to meeting the needs of married couples and their children.
• Pastors will ring doorbells of new residents in family-oriented housing developments and subdivisions in an effort to introduce themselves and extend invitations to Sunday services; but they make no effort to reach apartment-dwellers in the same parishes—particularly if the apartment complex is known to cater to singles.
• The ministers, being married themselves more often than not, simply find it easier to relate to other marrieds than to singles.

The overwhelming majority of active churchgoers simply do not realize how completely the married-couple-with-children-living-at-home has been made the norm of Christian life in America, feeling themselves to be acting out of sincere and well-placed concern for the well-being of the family unit.

It's a concern grounded in the Talmud Y'vomas, which states

that "any man who has no wife is not considered a full man."[9]

It continued to be a concern in Shakespeare's time, as is apparent from these lines in *King John:*

> He is the half part of a blessed man
> Left to be finished by such as she;
> And she is a fair divided excellence,
> Whose fulness of perfection lies in him. (act 2, sc. 1, lines 437–440)

Modern defenders of the church's sustenance and support of the model family—even at the expense of the single adult—use the words of Jesus as related in the New Testament section of the marriage service to disarm their critics: "Have ye not read, that he which made them at the beginning made them male and female, And said, For this cause shall a man leave father and mother, and shall cleave to his wife: and they twain shall be one flesh? Wherefore they are no more twain, but one flesh. What therefore God hath joined together, let not man put asunder" (Matt. 19:4–6).

Unfortunately, singles are hard-pressed to find an equally clear commandment to honor and respect the individual in his or her unmarried state, leaving them in want of spiritual enlightenment.

Marriage is eminently respectable in secular as well as religious society. It is a sanctified, legalized means of providing for the propagation of the species.

In the minds of many, a married man is a committed man, committed to a woman, a job, a community. A married woman eventually becomes a mother, committed to her family. As parents, they share a strong motivation to lead good Christian lives as examples for their children who, with the proper discipline and encouragement, will grow up to be husbands, wives, and parents themselves. This is the accepted cycle of Christian life.

And no one is attacking the family unit. It will and ought to remain crucial to the life of the church and the nation. But the

[9] *Talmud Y'vomas,* p. 63.

church, comprised as it is of family members, seems loath to admit that being unmarried is not an aberration from the Christian viewpoint; neither is marriage a commandment.

Some churches boast of having made special "accommodations" for young adult members, but folk services with guitars, drums, and trombones do not demonstrate genuine acceptance. They merely provide temporary relief from boredom for the regular churchgoer. Coffee houses, films, and debates only serve to pacify the few already there.

The existence of nearly fifty million unmarried adults in our society—one single for every married couple—should be sufficient to justify a major review, evaluation, and revision as to the form, structure, and nature of Christian life in the twentieth century.

Of course, there will be many obstacles along the way. For instance:

Clergymen are afraid. Ministers want to be thought of as open and understanding at all times, but they are fearful of the hard questions often asked by singles, for whom the standard "Because the Bible says so" is no longer an acceptable response to "But why?"

They are afraid that the single member will stir up their peaceful congregations and, in some cases, are secretly envious and jealous of the freedoms single people seem to enjoy.

They fantasize about the single life-style rather than attempting to establish relationships with singles that might lead to understanding. Astonishingly, it appears that few clergymen have ever admitted truly open, one-to-one relationships of this type into their busy, "other-directed" lives.

In a two-and-one-half-year study of the status of the laity in twenty-nine Chicago-area congregations, Dr. Elmer Witt discovered that none of the pastors considered any of their congregants to be "friends." None of the participating laity put their pastor(s) in the friend category either. Upon further probing, the pastors individually revealed that while they felt "closer" to some colleagues and former classmates than others they really had no close friends. Of the total, only two said they considered their wives to be "friends," and they were also perceived to be more open than the rest in their ministries of, by, for, through, and with the laity.

"My personal contention," concluded Dr. Witt, "is that most of these clergy (no women included in this sample), because of personality traits, or religious teaching, or by choice, had not experienced a deep, open relationship, i.e., a friendship, with *anyone.*"

Clergymen keep themselves at far too great a distance from the everyday working person in the business world.

Clergymen are suspicious. They imagine that someone might be having a good time. There is a genuine inability to smile, relax, and have fun, particularly among the Protestant devout, as anecdotes about the grim, unbending sobriety of archetypical Protestants indicate. As one Catholic archbishop recalls, "My grandmother could pick them out of a crowd. She used to say, 'She's got a Protestant face, that one.' Meaning, no joy." One is reminded of Grant Wood's famous *American Gothic,* depicting the New England farmer, cum pitchfork, and his pioneer-stock, unsmiling wife.

Clergymen demand too much churchiness. My building, *my* priorities, *my* program, *my* congregation, *my* flock. People unable to buy into this thought pattern are rejected.

Clergymen unwittingly submit to self-captivity in their endeavors to dominate and control rather than to liberate. They tend to equate control and power with "strength" and the lack of them with "weakness," which is not always the axiom it seems. Thus some would rather keep their congregation's growth "in check" than risk its expansion to "uncontrollable proportions."

Clergymen are far too preoccupied with the business of the church. That's all many clerics know, and to approach a person on any other basis is to threaten him or her.

Clergymen avoid pain. The church has become a bromide rather than a vehicle for helping people to recognize crises, to face their tensions and anxieties squarely, and to overcome them. Too often the church dispenses solace through parables and clichés; too seldom does it empathize with the sufferer.

With such clergymen as the "key" personalities in many Christian congregations and their most visible representatives in the surrounding community, it's no wonder that modern churches are beset by problems.

The most profound failure of the church has been its unwillingness to deal with situations at hand, to be real, helpful, and compassionate now. Not later, not when things change. Not after the prodigal sons come to realize the errors of their own ways and come crawling back repentant.

Church leaders seem to fear that change and accommodation would bring a corresponding loss to the religious and spiritual life, that people won't come to worship services, won't remain active as church members, if we admit open, honest discussions of our feelings and sexual needs. Instead they rely on rules and unbending doctrine to keep the flock in line. Actually, the way people live, love, and relate to one another has little to do with legal or religious ritual.

Divorce, liberalism, a new wave of intellectualism, the feminist movement, relaxed attitudes toward sex, overpopulation, and social and political injustice are chisels chipping away at the traditional pillars of the church.

No longer can the church be permitted to cleave to the past for its own sake. People and issues require solutions *now*.

4. The Wall Between

Something there is that doesn't love a wall,
That sends the frozen-ground-swell under it
And spills the upper boulders in the sun,
And makes gaps even two can pass abreast.

Something there is that doesn't love a wall,
That wants it down. . . .[10]

I had no way of foreseeing the chain of events that would lead to
my impassioned involvement in a most unusual kind of ministry
back in 1971. I had no way of knowing that I would be scaling
walls, displacing boulders as I went. In May 1971 I accepted a
"pastor to youth" position at St. Mark Church in Mt. Prospect,
Illinois, and the first small stone was dislodged.

It all began with a rather selfish reluctance on my part to live in
the parsonage next door to the church.

Even a minister feels the need to get away on his day off and
relax or study in solitude. As an ex-seminarian I'd been looking
forward to the time when as a gainfully employed young adult I

[10]From "Mending Wall" from *The Poetry of Robert Frost* edited by Edward Con-
nery Latham. Copyright 1930, 1939, © 1969 by Holt, Rinehart and Winston.
Copyright © 1958 by Robert Frost. Copyright © 1967 by Lesley Frost Ballan-
tine. Reprinted by permission of Holt, Rinehart and Winston, Publishers.

might begin to enjoy some of the amenities I'd long done without—an indoor swimming pool, for instance.

Fortunately, the congregation was willing to go along with me on this. They would rent out the parsonage, they decided, and appropriate the rental income to me for a housing allowance. "Go ahead," I was told indulgently, "and find a place where you can swim."

Obviously, my housing allowance wouldn't have covered a house with its own pool; so I began looking into apartment complexes, which also offered the contemporary, attractive, and relatively maintenance-free environment that I as a bachelor found appealing.

Within three days, I'd zeroed in on International Village in Schaumburg, Illinois, which was renting commodious one-bedroom apartments with access to a clubhouse and pool. The prices were well within my modest budget.

The management seemed amused that I, a Lutheran minister, was actually planning to live in what was widely known throughout the area as a singles complex. But within a week of the day I moved in, the management utilized my presence by referring a distressed resident to me who was seeking advice in dealing with an urgent, personal crisis in his life.

The next week, I was asked to perform a wedding. As I expanded my circle of personal acquaintants, exchanging pleasantries and making friends with my new neighbors, I was asked to perform baptisms, several more weddings, and an ecumenical Thanksgiving meditation service with Rabbi Gershon Rosenstock. Gradually, I began to realize that there was potential in the complex itself for a full-time ministry. A void was not being filled by churches and synagogues in the surrounding communities. They had neither sought, nor been prevailed upon, to close the gap.

"Something there is that doesn't love a wall, That wants it down."

The idea grew and began to take shape.

I consulted with friends from St. Mark, with the bishop, the mission director, and several people from neighboring parishes as well as with the owner/developer of the apartment complex and his management staff. They were intrigued by the possibility of what we were already calling an "apartment ministry." We had heard that such things had been attempted in other cities on an experimental basis, and although the jury was still out in those experiments, we decided to give it a whirl.

On June 1, 1973, I resigned my post at St. Mark and accepted a Letter of Call to become the full-time pastor of New Apartment Ministry at International Village.

Full of enthusiasm, I moved into a two-bedroom apartment and set about converting the spare room into an office. My work, from this point on, would be right at home, in one of 760 apartments on a sprawling forty-nine-acre tract that was also home to twelve hundred other residents, most of them singles. A suburban Chicago singles complex was to be my new parish.

Norman J. Ackerberg, the developer of this and four other apartment complexes in Bloomington, Minnesota, Lombard, Illinois, Bolingbrook, Illinois, and Fort Lauderdale, Florida, responded so enthusiastically to a live-in resident minister that in addition to providing me with rent-free quarters and some office assistance he enlarged the scope of the ministry to include all five complexes. Picking up the tab for my frequent travel expenses, he liked to chuckle, "Pastor Nic, you've got one of the largest parishes in the country."

At the outset, I had more questions than answers, more problems than solutions, but I was quickly caught up in an exciting new adventure. I was jetting around the country, meeting hundreds of new people, developing some interesting programs, and coming to the attention of the local news-hounds. Some publicity in the local newspapers led to a guest appearance on a nationally televised morning talk show.

The excitement I felt seemed to be infectious. My relations with neighboring congregations were encouraging; pastors and parishioners visited International Village and attended some of the "rap sessions" I'd begun holding on a regular basis. The entire North Chicago Pastor's Conference scheduled one of its regular monthly meetings at the complex. In other cities, church and civic groups followed suit.

Gaps were opening in the seemingly impregnable walls that had long kept established churches and young singles at a respectful distance from each other. In what can only be described as a state of euphoria, I sensed that the community outside was reaching in and that the community within the complex was maturing and reaching out.

But the wall had merely been penetrated and not torn down, as I discovered two months into the ministry.

The real breakthrough, when it came, intruded on my own consciousness, eroding that euphoric sensation in which all had seemed to be going so well. At the same time it steered me toward what Robert Frost had also anticipated in one of his poems: "the road not taken." And that, with a grateful nod toward the poet, "has made all the difference."

During one of those grueling "creative sessions" in which I'd been composing the Sunday sermon to a typical suburban church, I found myself mentally fatigued and in need of a break. Leaving my office, I jogged over to the local coffee shop, ordered a snack, and gobbled it down. Refreshed and in a hurry to get back to work, I stood at the cashier's booth, waiting impatiently for my change, when a gentleman I had never seen before approached.

"You're Pastor Nic, aren't you?" he asked tentatively.

"Yes, I am!"

"I really need to talk to you. I've got a pressing problem . . ."

"Sure. Fine! How about tomorrow sometime?"

"I guess that'll be OK," he stammered.

"See you."

I never saw him again.

That experience forced me to come to grips with the real purpose of my apartment ministry. I wasn't there to write sermons, travel, languish in my apartment, or receive jollies from local headlines and TV guest shots. As a live-in minister, I had a serious responsibility to listen to and help the residents who needed help, in the same way the pastor of a church should be hearing and meeting needs of the congregation. I was a missionary. By my presence, I was supposed to demonstrate to the residents that the church cares about them, about their struggles and their joys, and that the church wants to help when it is asked to do so. Without my unquestioning acceptance of and availability to the resident in need, I realized with a shock, my ministry was without value.

In crystallizing this insight I began to understand that I too had been guilty of building and mending walls, and I resolved to begin clawing at boulders with renewed vigor.

From that time on, I made a point of being casually available at nearly every activity in International Village—swimming parties, brunches, tennis matches, and Friday-night get-togethers. I began to know my fellow residents, to understand the pressures and promises from which the fabric of their lives was woven. I listened to what they had to say. The feeling that I really belonged came upon me. I had come into my own, and everything fell into place.

Even my occasional sentimental reminiscences of the first year in Louisiana, when I was pastor of my own church, receded into proper perspective and balance.

This new apartment ministry was not only the worthwhile venture I had always believed it could be. It was also a crucial foray which could be of extreme importance to the church someday.

The church needed to develop and discover ways of reaching the thousands of walled-in apartment residents across the country. Apartments are everywhere, and everywhere are occupants with unmet personal, psychological, and spiritual needs.

The importance and urgency of these discoveries gave my

work added significance and a compelling motivation: I would not only develop the skills crucial to operating a successful apartment ministry, but I would somehow convey those skills and my sense of urgency in adapting and enlarging upon them to the church at large.

5. Apartment Ministry in Action

The absence of a model for an apartment ministry, of a cut-and-dried guideline to follow, turned out to be a blessing. It forced me to trust my own judgment and instinct in deriving solutions that flowed from common sense. I had to roll with the punches and let the ministry happen. This freedom, flexibility, and exploration led me to discover abundant resources of strength, support, and eventually an effective pragmatic style for ministry.

I leaned on the people that stood behind my work. Bishop Elmer Nelson, mission director Donald Johnson, attorney Jack Davis, and Pastor Jim Kragness were my "core four," listening, counseling, and lending a hand whenever needed.

This support base grew. Within a year more than twenty-five dedicated supporters formed a special apartment ministry steering committee. This committee—composed of church people, apartment dwellers, neighboring singles, and friends—provided a forum for discussion of new ideas, evaluation of ongoing programs, and a base of continuing support.

Together we discussed our goals and decided that my first objective should be availability on a continuing, casual basis. After some reflection, we also concluded that if there were no model there was at least a starting point of reference.

This ministry was to be one of conversation, much like that of a chaplain in the armed services and hospitals. Interest in the resident as a person was to be genuine, without intent to change him or her or provide unwanted advice. I would be there to listen, to care, and to respond.

The armed forces chaplaincy system has been around a long time. Now in its 202nd year of existence, it was formed one year before the birth of our nation, in 1775, at the urging of regimental commanders in the thirteen developing colonies who perceived a need for it. Then, and now, it was their philosophy that whenever persons are taken away from their usual surroundings or home environment, particularly if there is a chance they may be sent to war, the government has an obligation to ease the trauma in every way possible. Those who had been taken away from their churches deserved an opportunity to receive spiritual support in the camps and on the battlefield, the government decided, taking great pains however to make sure that it remained an *opportunity* and not a requirement.

The objective of the chaplains then as now was to:

- Provide "traditional" worship services for those who wished to take advantage of them;
- Remain open to innovations that would make the program more meaningful to the particular population being served, in this case, the armed forces;
- Foster specialization through advanced training so that there would be chaplains sensitive to the special problems and requirements of the hospitalized and imprisoned; and
- Keep in mind the welfare of the total community through availability to nonbelievers as well as churchgoing soldiers.

"The program," says Col. Albert F. Ledebuhr, senior chaplain, U.S. Army, at Fort Monroe, Virginia, "produces better soldiers. And a better soldier means a better and stronger defense system for the protection of our country."

There's a spiritual payoff as well. "There is more ecumenism in the military," says Ledebuhr, "than anywhere else. I have learned that we are all brothers in the faith. We are all the recipients of God's love."

With these guidelines in mind, and the need to tailor my ministry specifically to the single adults displaced from their home environments, these innovations were adopted:

• Personal and confidential counseling via the telephone or by appointment. I was available on a one-to-one basis to anyone who requested it.

• Referral to doctors, hospitals, lawyers, or other professionals and to the local churches or synagogues for those who requested the information.

• Causal meditation meetings in which residents could gather for informal worship and prayer. These were always conducted on an ecumenical level for those who did not have a church home in which to meet periodically, establish new friendships, and worship God.

I designed special "Worship Alternative" cards to distribute as announcements of these meetings. When I discuss worship or church with new residents or other people I call on, I present them with a Worship Alternative card. This serves as a reminder and reference to me as well as to other area ministers whose names are listed on the cards.

Special worship alternatives are scheduled throughout the year which incorporate creative expressions of religious commitment. One such special worship alternative, held at 6 o'clock on Easter morning at a Chicago hotel, included a ballet company's interpretation of the death and resurrection of Christ.

• Weddings. I always refer engaged couples to their home church or the denominational church in the community. But when those who have developed a close relationship with me through the ministry specifically requested my services, I obliged.

• Bible classes for interested residents. My most enjoyable

ministerial function is teaching the Bible. I designed a special study series based on the personalities of the Gospel writers. I would reflect upon Luke, for example, a Greek physician who saw Jesus as the perfect man who came to heal, seek, and save the lost.

Levi the tax collector who was hated because he served the Romans at the expense of his fellow Jews became the writer of the first book of the New Testament.

Mark, the Roman who appealingly bids his fellow Romans to see Jesus as the mighty, wonder-working servant of God, stands in interesting contrast to John, who writes much later and was one of Jesus' closest disciples.

Apartment residents in today's society appreciate relating to the Biblical saints on a personal, comparative level.

I conduct such classes in my apartment and at neighboring churches. Past experiences have indicated that these informative but casual studies have been an effective way to bring together active and non-active church-goers.

• Rap sessions on timely topics. This provided a stimulating and enjoyable alternative to the bar scene for singles interested in meeting other singles. When the movie *The Exorcist* was popular, I brought in a priest who had performed an exorcism to discuss the subject. Doctors, lawyers, celebrities, hypnotists, rabbis, and congressmen all participated in other rap sessions in which people met people on a casual basis.

• Wine and cheese parties. Young adults who were loath to participate in the bar or disco scene seemed to consider these an acceptable alternative.

• Availability through visibility. Frequently this meant being at the swimming pool or the tennis courts when large groups gathered, striking up conversations in the local grocery store, making myself known to as many people as possible in the environments most frequented by the residents.

While I avoid imposing myself upon a situation, I never deliberately hide my identity. I dress appropriately for the occasion. I can be seen in my clerical collar, actually looking like a minister, when I am on the way to a gathering that requires clerical wardrobe. I wear the collar for Sunday morning services, hospital calls, and occasionally when I have no other clean clothes available. My occupation and purpose is recognizable even when I dress in lay clothes because I am more often than not inviting someone to a wine and cheese party or a rap session, or presenting them with my Worship Alternative card.

In addition to all these things, I somehow found the time, because it seemed so important, to conduct apartment ministry workshops for interested pastors and laity, to write and circulate an apartment ministry newsletter, to accept invitations to preach at local churches, and to address singles groups throughout the country.

As the work progressed, my support base grew, abetted by letters of appreciation from people I'd counseled or married, growing participation in my TA classes and rap sessions, administrative assistance by enthusiastic volunteers, and nationwide curiosity about how the project was getting along. For a while, it seemed as though every newspaper reporter planning a piece on singles would call and pick my brain. As a result, my bishop and mission director were willing to continue the financial support so crucial to the survival of any ministry.

Innovations continued to develop. For example, the large sale of Dr. Thomas Harris's book *I'm OK—You're OK* and the popularity of the human potential movement provided a natural opportunity to expand my personal and confidential counseling into growth group sessions. Subsequently, I joined the International Transactional Analysis Association (ITAA) as a regular member and became an understudy of Dr. Bill Goerss of Park Ridge, Illinois. I was dually qualified to lead groups—first, as a pastor of the American Lutheran Church; second, according to the provisions prescribed by ITAA.

Human potential growth-groups based on the principles of Transactional Analysis (TA) became an integral part of my work. TA is not to be confused with TM (transcendental meditation) or with any of the gamut of self-improvement schemes that have been put forward in the "Me" generation. TA, or Transactional Analysis, is a common-sense way of getting to know ourselves and others better. The goal is to feel OK.

Eric Berne, who first introduced the term *Transactional Analysis* into the language more than a decade ago with his best-selling book *Games People Play,* believed that too many basically OK people were entering therapy or psychoanalysis as "patients"; in other words, they perceived themselves as not OK and in need of a cure. But to fall prey to occasional depression or to feel in a rut is not a disease, not even unusual; to eliminate permanently the possibility that depression will recur is impossible. Therefore, he reasoned, any "cure" is illusory.

For those people not mentally ill but rather trying to change some unsatisfactory habit or pattern which interfered with their fullest enjoyment of life, Berne attempted to provide support and a mechanism for dealing with everyday upsets, in other words, a way to cope.

TA, it seemed to me, was a tool that could be used by the church as well as by individuals in coping with the frustrations and upsets that come along and as a tool for change. It seemed particularly helpful to a minister trying to find new ways of relating to people who felt left out.

TA stresses the importance of being "straight" with other people; that is, it is crucial to ask frankly and directly for whatever you want of a person without playing games.

It's not difficult to picture a church council or congregation much improved and enriched by an application of such principles. Properly understood, they are another way of stating the commandments—honesty, love for one's neighbor, honor, respect.

What's more, I found that many singles who had been turned off by "churchiness" quickly got turned on by TA's good sense, moral outlook, and refusal to condemn them for what they were not. Some were not willing to admit it, but in almost every case they were looking for some sort of direction, a sense of purpose, some moral guidance. That's what they found in TA.

Human potential growth-groups based on TA were formed, and by a vote of the first group to sign up, decided to meet in my apartment one evening each week. There we could relax in comfortable, nonthreatening surroundings and speak our minds.

Residents signed up for a five-or-ten-week period in which they received instruction in the simple mechanics of TA and were taught to role-play troublesome dialogues. Liking themselves better, the first group of "graduates" passed the word to others. Before I knew it, I was teaching two classes, two nights a week, and counseling several others on a one-to-one basis.

Some, impressed by the fact that a minister was providing what seemed to be an effective instrument in their daily lives, began to ask timid, then increasingly probing questions about the correlation of TA to theology. Several books have been written on the subject, and undoubtedly, several more will appear. For me, TA made a strong plank in the bridge I was trying to build between two worlds—church people and the single adult.

A thirty-one-year-old Jewish writer, who had not set foot inside a synagogue in years, thanked me for opening her eyes to the "potential" of religion although we had never discussed religion per se in the class. Some months after completing the course, she confided to me that it had instilled in her a desire to reach out to new people and experiences and to reach back into her roots for a better understanding of herself. As a result, she had sought out and found a rabbi who had been willing to spend long hours reacquainting her with the basics of Jewish law: how to prepare for Passover, how to recite the blessing over the Sabbath candles, how to pronounce the Hebrew liturgy, and so forth.

"Some of my friends think I've gone off the deep end," she admitted with a chuckle, "but I feel more OK than I ever have. I wanted to share that with you."

I was deeply moved.

She and others who reported similar experiences said they had been able to add "texture" or "depth" to their lives. I think that is an accurate assessment of what happened. Another way of putting it is that they began to celebrate life itself, which led to an almost inevitable search for the Creator although some preferred to use the terms *spirit, guiding force, higher power.*

I was frequently tempted to proselytize, to tell the non-Christian to examine the life of Jesus. If asked to discuss the teachings of my church, I was only too happy to oblige. I was never bashful about my faith, but I was cautious about becoming too parochial, about seeing any of these people as not-OK, a mistake that could only interfere with our ability to relate effectively and meaningfully to one another.

There were other concerns: What about singles who were not interested in getting into anything so structured as a regular Wednesday-night class? What about those who had resigned themselves to, or even embraced, a non-OK type of existence?

For them, I made myself available in other settings and at other times of the day. I passed the word that my door is always open, that I could be called at any hour of the day or night. Frequently I was jangled into consciousness by a 3 A.M. phone call from a troubled resident: "Are you awake? I just need somebody to talk to."

Everybody needs somebody to talk to. To my surprise, some singles were more inclined to confide in a friendly and available minister—even a minister of a faith different from their own—than in a close friend or relative. "My mother is too involved in her own problems" was one phrase I heard a lot. "How could I ever tell my priest [or boyfriend or ex-wife, etc.]?" was another.

My greatest value, I came to realize, was as a sounding board and, occasionally, as a conduit to other pastors, health care, community, or service organizations. "You're the only person I know," a twenty-four-year-old homosexual in Chicago told me, "who will listen without condemning."

Unfortunately, that wasn't all there was to it. Some frustrations developed. Pastors unfamiliar with nontraditional ministries sometimes fail to understand that a pastor like myself is no less dedicated or hard-working than themselves.

"What do you do all day anyway?" is a question that used to come up a lot when groups of us got together. It was a question guaranteed to give me a headache because it seemed based on the assumption that a ministry is not really a ministry unless it's built around the world of Sunday morning sermons and Word and sacraments.

But the question deserves an answer, and here it is. Writing reports, letters, sermons, doing research, organizing programs, planning classes, contacting speakers for special events, and publishing newsletters are some of the other chores that I can't escape. Work left to church councils, parish committees, or paid office workers in more conventional kinds of ministries is the pastor's alone in this type of ministry. With the generosity of a particularly sympathetic bishop or apartment owner, it's sometimes possible to secure the help of a part-time clerical helper, but rarely are there funds available for more than one additional salary. Despite the willingness of some residents to lick stamps or stuff envelopes on occasion, the responsibility for getting things done is the pastor's alone.

These administrative tasks can be unbearably time-consuming, taking you away from the people you're trying to serve, which is a never-ending source of frustration.

Another source of frustration was the initial skepticism expressed by other church people about how this odd ministry of mine would "fit into" their scheme of things. Interestingly, several of these early skeptics joined the steering committee out of curiosity and have emerged as some of my strongest advocates.

It was not surprising to me that when church people observed the programmed activities firsthand and listened to residents tell how meaningful this ministry was their support would follow. The message communicated in all this was that the church really *cares* and *does* want to help wherever and whenever help is needed. Subsequently, singles would begin to be more encouraged to think positively about the church and even consider attending Sunday morning services once again.

After four full years, I still regard my apartment ministry as being in the experimental stage since changes and innovations continue to be made as we go along and find a better way of doing something. There is more to be learned, and only a few conclusions can be drawn from what has already transpired.

Several such conclusions can be summarized as follows:

1. Apartment ministry works. To make it work, the synod, district, or congregation must be willing to program its success. It's that simple.
2. A minister's approach must be down-to-earth and human to be effective among laity. In other words, one must understand one's relationship with sin and grace in order to be effective in this work.
3. An ecumenical approach is crucial.
4. The utmost concern of an apartment ministry should be to demonstrate the love of God to people, emphasizing that the church really cares. It should not merely be viewed as a vehicle to recruit people into the local church. As Grace Ann Goodman pointed out in a 1968 study *The Church and the Apartment House—Case Studies,* churches that see the apartment minister as their agent to "reach" previously closed territory are usually unwilling to change their attitudes toward newcomers or adapt their programs to other

life-styles.[11] The responsibility for recruitment and welcoming those who attend a worship service for the first time is and should remain the responsibility of the church itself.

5. Singles are whole, complete individuals regardless of their marital status. In other words, they are OK and must be accepted as such before any meaningful dialogue can take place.[12]

6. The media are interested in the activities of the church, and the media can be a valuable tool in informing singles what services are available. Churches usually shy away from the media so as not to appear that they are bragging, but an excess of "humility" can also be a sin.

[11] Grace Ann Goodman, *The Church and the Apartment House—Case Studies* (New York: United Presbyterian Church U.S.A., Board of National Missions, 1968), p. 84.

[12] See Appendix A pp. 131ff. for a continuum of well-being for 48,926,000 singles.

6. What Ails Singles:
Seven Deadly Sins

In the course of my work with singles from Minnesota to Florida, I began to be struck by the similarity of the problems they brought to our rap sessions and therapy workshops. Concerns serious enough to cause a twenty-four-year-old Bloomington, Minnesota, bachelor deep personal anguish, interfering with his performance at work and hampering the development of satisfying relationships with his peer group, would be expressed a week later in almost identical terms by an unmarried, thirty-five-year-old woman in Fort Lauderdale. Elderly widowers in Chicago, "swinging" bachelors in suburban Schaumburg, schoolteachers in New York, and social workers in Denver related the same worries so often that I began to wonder if the causes weren't the same also.

To the happily married pastor who persists in seeing bachelorhood as the ailment and marriage as the cure, some of these problems may seem trivial, even trite. But to the young men and women who came to me, sometimes in tears, sometimes on the verge of suicide, they were a source of pervasive despair and an admission of defeat. To many of them, the remote possibility that I might be able to help them out of their ruts and through the rough times loomed as a court of last resort.

Over and over again, they complained of deep-seated and unrelieved depression, loneliness, boredom, and hopelessness. They bemoaned the lack of loving relationships in their lives, shallow friendships, and not being able to "find" themselves. They talked about not being able to "fit in" anywhere, not being able to accomplish the goals for which they yearned, of not being willing to "settle" for the colorless lives being led by their parents.

"If it weren't for my boss" they'd begin, or "my girlfriend" or "my debts" or "my skinny legs." In the course of 441 counseling sessions with unmarried men and women over a two-year period, it became obvious to me that the real causes lay much deeper.

Laziness, lack of purpose, selfishness, lack of honesty, the failure to take risks, allowing oneself to be overwhelmed and overcome by setbacks, and *the failure to take God seriously* were at the root of so many physical, emotional, financial, and spiritual problems that I began to recognize these seven commonplace transgressions as the "invisible" culprits in most cases. I call them the "seven deadly sins" to which single adults are particularly vulnerable. Recognizing them is more than fifty percent of the solution.

1. LAZINESS

The single person living alone is prone to laziness in every degree. In the absence of outside pressure to tidy up the house, launder one's clothes, and keep the refrigerator stocked with nutritious foods, one is apt to take "Don't do it today unless you can't put it off until tomorrow" for a motto. Whether out of sheer laziness, obstinacy, or exhaustion, some singles refuse to make the most of a free weekend; they have only themselves to blame if boredom and depression set in.

Take John, for example, for whom boredom and depression are common complaints. It's finally Saturday, his day off. He sleeps a few hours later than usual. Skips breakfast because he doesn't have a clean dish in the house. Turns on television to catch the afternoon college football game. Resists calling a friend for an evening date because that would entail a shave and a clean shirt. Gets by on a few beers, stale pretzels, and some week-old Polish sausage, and winds up the evening by himself, watching "Saturday Night Live."

Single persons who allow themselves to be ruled by lethargy often become too lazy to increase their circle of friends—who can be vitally important to their sense of well-being.

Single persons often become too lazy to strive for the better, higher-paying job through which they could experience personal gratification and a real sense of accomplishment. Before they know it, perhaps without even realizing it, they've developed a pessimistic, "what's the use?" attitude about life in general. Their ability to retain old friends, jobs, even a minimal amount of self-respect is seriously endangered.

The saintly virtue that counters the deadly sin of laziness is motivation. More often than not, a swift kick in the pants would suffice. Motivation is essential to cultivating healthy self-image and to attaining goals that will bring the prestige, recognition, and personal gratification so earnestly desired. Once motivated to pursue physical and intellectual development with all the vigor at one's disposal, the single person becomes a fuller, happier, more interesting, and more lovable individual. He or she is someone who can be fun, and even inspiring, to be around. A single person can defeat laziness by the simple act of getting off one's duff and doing whatever needs to be done.

Suzanne Gordon, the author of *Lonely in America,* says she found it "frightening" to discover how much loneliness there is in this land. She calls loneliness, which happens to be a frequent byproduct of laziness, a chronic American ailment, a "mass social problem" brought on by the way we live. But the loneliness engendered by laziness is not without remedy. One need only face the cause squarely to get a glimmering of the usually all-too-obvious solution.

For example, a person to whom loneliness means an unbearably empty apartment, with no one to talk to, no one to share a meal with, no one to relieve the monotony of eating and falling asleep in front of the television set, the obvious solution is a roommate. Why hasn't he or she found a roommate? Because, all too often, he or she *hasn't even tried!* The obvious solution is to make a concerted effort by asking friends or co-workers to alert their friends and co-workers of his or her desire for a rommate. Place ads in the local newspapers, notices on bulletin boards, and an application in the files of one of the agencies springing up in major cities across the United States which specialize in matching up compatible roommates—often at no cost to the applicant with the apartment.

Sometimes, acquiring an affectionate pet from the local animal shelter will help fill the void for a person who lives alone. The act of giving and receiving love, even to a pet, can be a powerful antidote to loneliness and depression and a new source of delight in life.

Similarly, a single who complains of "having no way to meet people" may find a pleasing solution to this problem in night classes, volunteer work, special interest groups, parties, political activities, tennis or racquetball tournaments, or singles clubs. There are so many opportunities available to enrich the single life that it's really a shame to let laziness stand in one's way.

One friend of mine decided to hit the problem of laziness head-on. He enrolled in a gourmet cooking class. As his skills improved, he became eager to invite everyone he knew to dinner so that he could demonstrate his mastery of the culinary arts. Of course, that meant keeping the house in order, the fridge stocked with food, and the laundry from piling up in the hallway. To my friend's delight, he found laziness plaguing him less and less and his loneliness wiped out in the praise and camaraderie of his increasingly well-fed friends.

For a special New Year's Eve date, he served smoked sausages, homemade French onion soup, fresh salad, steak, asparagus in butter sauce, baked potato with cheese, coffee, flaming dessert crêpes, and, of course, the appropriate wines and champagnes. It was an evening the lucky lady is not apt to forget!

Another friend of mine simply got up, made a down payment on a baby grand piano, had it moved into his apartment, and began taking music lessons.

Most problems that singles complain about are not caused by inconsiderate parents, an irate boss, or the federal government. More often than not, they are brought about by the individual's personal decision to be lazy.

2. LACK OF PURPOSE / DESTINY

Serious problems occur among those who find no purpose and meaning in life or who simply fail to take life seriously. When singles choose living together over marriage, without weighing the consequences in terms of their ultimate goals, they are apt to court heartache and disaster.

Most often, success doesn't just happen. It's carefully planned.

For example, one doesn't become a Nadia Comaneci (Romania's eighty-six-pound Olympic idol) overnight. Nadia practices four hours every day, except Sundays. Any successful athlete, entertainer, musician, scientist, or businessman has to be prepared to make a similar investment in terms of time, labor, persistence, and dedication. Most happy, well-adjusted individuals are constantly setting new and realistic goals for themselves as they ascend the ladder of personal achievement.

Singles caught up in the social, moral, and economic tensions of our time can't afford to maintain a carefree attitude of letting nature take its course, particularly where decisions about sex and marriage are concerned. Sexual promiscuity may seem to offer an easy shortcut to the affection and attention we all crave, but if the ultimate goal is a loving and durable relationship, imbued with the honesty and integrity so crucial to a happy marriage, that particular shortcut may turn out to be a dead end.

Jerry Gillies, the author of *My Needs, Your Needs, Our Needs*, leads human potential workshops in Miami, Florida. He maintains that sheer physical pleasure in sexual gratification can't be compared to the heights one can experience in a feeling, caring relationship in which each partner is willing to let go. The whole "sexual-sensual interaction," Gillies told me, is entirely dependent on one's ability to let go, emotionally as well as physically, being fully alive and fully present.

It is seldom possible for people to reach the heights of fulfillment and satisfaction that Gillies talks about outside the realm of a deep personal and spiritual commitment. Without a sense of purpose, no "progress" can be seen to bring one nearer to a goal. Time goes by, but the individual has nothing to show for advanced age and accumulated experience and this leads to a loss of self-respect and to deep-seated depression.

The virtue required here is to establish one's purpose in life by setting and striving for realistic, meaningful goals.

You could start by allowing yourself to dream of the things that you would really like to have happen to you in your lifetime. List ten specific things that you must accomplish or sincerely want out of life. For example: to be happily married, to earn twenty-five thousand dollars a year, to live near the Pacific Ocean, to own your own home, to complete a college education, to write a book, to save more money, to become a happier person, to contribute to society in a meaningful way.

It's a matter of evaluating one's situation in life, focusing on one's uppermost aspirations and desires, and setting serious goals to accomplish the desired result:

1. Begin immediately by taking one small step. Write out your goals. Set time limits in which to achieve them.
2. Follow through completely.
3. Enjoy and celebrate your little successes and accomplishments.
4. Keep your direction and goal in mind at all times.
5. Advance to bigger goals.
6. Become committed to accomplishing your goals.

3. SELFISHNESS

Singles are more prone to the sin of selfishness than their married counterparts. They can afford to be more selfish with their leisure time, money, and personal belongings. Such inner-directed attention leaves one virtually bankrupt of the enrichment to be derived from giving of one's self.

Americans spend approximately $146 billion a year on leisure activities;[13] the ad writers would have us believe that it will take a new set of golf clubs, the right kind of tennis racket, and the latest model sports car to experience fully the joys life has in store for us. Some singles stay in debt up to their ears in a struggle to possess those things, in their selfish craving for pleasure. Thus, time and money, their two most potent resources, are carelessly and selfishly directed on pursuits that have little relation, if any, to their ultimate goals.

Time and money can also be shared with friends and relations, however, or applied to the fulfillment of "ultimate" goals—an education, a career, personal advancement and fulfillment.

People who do not allow themselves to be swerved from their purpose in life by selfish, short-range indulgences tend to have more friends and, above all, a better attitude about themselves.

To give of one's self does not result in a loss of identity, personality, or individuality. To give of one's self is to share who and what you are. It's an extension, rather than a loss, of self. For the truly unselfish person, the rewards are an inner glow of satisfaction and an outward appearance of being a person who is nice to know.

Furthermore, doctors and psychologists have discovered that people who have specific responsibilities, commitments, and friendships with other people do not become as ill or require

---

[13] William L. MacDougall, "How Americans Pursue Happiness," *U.S. News & World Report* LXXXII, no. 20 (May 23, 1977), p. 62.

treatment as often as those who are free from such responsibilities and attachments.

Unselfishness brings about a greater sensitivity to life itself and contributes to real self-discovery and personal awareness. One becomes healthy in mind, body, and soul by reaching out and touching others.

In *Why Am I Afraid to Tell You Who I Am?* a book about insights, self-awareness, personal growth, and interpersonal communication, John Powell writes:

> The fully human person is in deep and meaningful contact with the world outside him.
>
> He not only listens to himself, but to the voices of his world. The breadth of his own individual experience is infinitely multiplied through a sensitive empathy with others. He suffers with the suffering, rejoices with the joyful. He is born again in every Springtime, feels the impact of the great mysteries of life: birth, growth, love, suffering, death. His heart skips along with the "young lovers," and he knows something of the exhilaration that is in them. He also knows the ghetto's philosophy of despair, the loneliness of suffering without relief, and the bell never tolls without tolling in some strange way for him. [14]

4. LACK OF HONESTY

Singles play games and wear masks. The bars are full of people projecting false personalities on unsuspecting persons who take them at face value. Not surprisingly, such relationships often falter.

Some singles play the game over and over again, reaping one disappointment after another in relationships with people they'd been hoping to dupe or impress; yet they seem unable or unwilling to change. Why is it necessary to assume a role that is not really

---

[14]John Powell, *Why Am I Afraid to Tell You Who I Am?* (Chicago: Argus Communications Co., 1960), p. 100.

you when confronted with an opportunity to increase your circle of friends?

Some say it's because they are frightened to "open up" to a stranger, because they haven't been honest with *themselves* and in touch with their own feelings, because "people don't believe you when you're honest," or because honesty can lead to rejection.

Perhaps it *is* easier, at least initially, to pretend to be somebody you're not than to face up to your real self. But to experience acceptance as you really are is a very important and enormously warming human experience.

Good friends usually relate to one another in a truthful, sincere, open manner. Single people would do well to apply the candor that comes naturally in dealing with friends to all the others who pass through their lives.

A lack of honesty causes people to love things and use people, rather than to use things and love people, in what John Powell terms "the death warrant for happiness and human fulfillment."[15] The most serious byproduct of dishonesty is a snowball effect in which the game becomes more real than reality and the player becomes unable to trust anyone. Dishonest persons always lose in the end. They lose the trust of the people to whom they want to get close; they lose their ability to trust in others; and they are also bound to misplace their self-respect and personal integrity somewhere along the way.

Honesty takes courage. The fears that lead a person to seek refuge behind a mask are vividly described by an anonymous poet:

> Don't be fooled by me.
> Don't be fooled by the face I wear.
> For I wear a mask, I wear a thousand masks.
> Masks that I'm afraid to take off.
> And none of them are me.

[15] John Powell, p. 49.

Pretending is an art that's second nature to me.
But don't be fooled, for God's sake don't be fooled.
I give you the impression that I'm secure,
That all is sunny and unruffled with me,
Within as well as without,
that confidence is my name and coolness my game,
that the water's calm and I'm in command,
and that I need no one.

But don't believe me.
Please.

My surface may seem smooth, but my surface is my mask.
My ever-varying and ever-concealing mask.
Beneath lies no smugness, no complacence
Beneath dwells the real me in confusion, in fear, in aloneness,
But I hide this.
I don't want anybody to know it.
I panic at the thought of my weakness and fear being exposed.
That's why I frantically create a mask to hide behind,
  A nonchalant, sophisticated façade to help me pretend, to shield me
    from the glance that knows. . . .

Some of us take refuge in dishonesty or deceit to protect ourselves from exposure, some to protect others from harsh or un-
pleasant truths. To be honest with one's self means having to
acknowledge one's mistakes as they become known. But as Harry
Browne points out in *How I Found Freedom in an Unfree World,* "If
you can accept your mistakes, you can correct them, pay for them,
learn from them and see that they don't interfere with your security." It's the person who can't acknowledge his or her errors
who "will remain vulnerable and be doomed to repeat them."[16]

Often, chronic dishonesty leads to even greater difficulties than
are averted by one's failure to tell the truth. For instance, the

---

[16] Harry Browne, *How I Found Freedom in an Unfree World* (New York: Mac-
millan, 1973), p. 219.

frequently dishonest person will be forced to cover up one lie with another to guard against discovery. He or she will forfeit rewarding relationships with people who would like the "real" person, but they never get to know what he or she is really like. The dishonest person becomes saddled with a massive load of guilt and insecurity, which can effectively prevent him or her from being able to relax and enjoy whatever "benefit" may have been reaped by lying in the first place.

Your friends deserve you at your best—open, honest, and sensitive. You owe yourself the same truthfulness.

5. FAILURE TO TAKE RISKS

Many people remain unmarried because they fear the risks involved, choosing to "Rather bear those ills we have Than fly to others that we know not of" as Shakespeare's Hamlet, one bachelor who met a tragic end, so eloquently expressed it.

The ten risks most frequently cited by singles as too frightening to justify marriage involve:

1. Loss of freedom.
2. The additional family responsibility should children become involved.
3. Opening oneself to a commitment that might fail.
4. Fear that the partners may develop divergent interests and grow apart.
5. Facing the unknown.
6. In-laws.
7. Sexual fears.
8. For divorced persons, the risk of being "twice-burned."
9. Unfaithfulness.
10. Financial sacrifice.

To be sure, there are no guarantees—in marriage or in any of life's other ventures or adventures. A successful marriage, like a successful business partnership, requires careful planning, a willingness to compromise, a commitment to success, and the mutual trust, respect, and caring of each partner.

That time-worn expression, "Nothing ventured, nothing gained," became an adage because over the years so many people found it to be true.

To risk is to admit the possibility of failure. But a risk-taker can increase the chances of success substantially by taking on the responsibility needed to produce the desired result and by investing the time, energy, and whatever temporary sacrifices may be required to turn a risk into an exciting and rewarding adventure.

The saintly virtue needed to counter the sin of failure to take risks is confidence. Babe Ruth was notorious at striking out, but because he had the confidence to try and try again, he is best remembered as a home-run slugger. Confidence is an acquired virtue, which can be strengthened through the use of a few simple exercises:

1. Begin with an honest evaluation of your potential. Are you overqualified for the job you now hold? Then you may be qualified to fill the opening in another department you so covet but have been afraid to "risk" applying for.

2. Give yourself permission to tap your resources of mind and spirit. If it's marriage you see as a "hopeless risk," you could test your ability to cope with the possibility of failure on a much smaller scale. Invite your prospective in-laws over for supper, for instance, at the risk of discovering they are the fault-finding ogres who would make your married life miserable. If they turn out to be disarmingly nice people, you'll have reduced the risk of marriage. If they turn out to be monsters, you may be surprised at your ability to take their criticisms with a grain of salt and resist their attempts to dampen your spirit.

3. Allow yourself the right to make a few mistakes while working toward your goal. None of us is infallible. A sense of humor

and a healthy respect for your ability to bounce back with renewed vigor will help.

4. Don't minimize your past accomplishments. List them. Look
at your list. Dwell on them. Praise yourself for them. Celebrate
them. An employee who is aware of having succeeded at every
assigned task doesn't hesitate to ask for more challenging tasks,
with correspondingly greater rewards. A woman who has successfully conquered the temptation to bite her fingernails may
decide to stop smoking as her next project. A person "in touch
with" past successes tends to be a happy person, confident of
future success.

5. Love yourself. When you love someone else, the very act of
doing something to make him or her happy can pay you back in
spades, with a deep, warm glow of personal satisfaction. The
same holds true of those who love themselves. You can almost
always make yourself happier than you are by daring to risk the
security that comes from being "just all right." To love yourself is
to feel you're entitled to the best that life has to offer, to all the fun
that goes along with making the most of yourself. Have you put
off taking tennis lessons at the risk of appearing gawky or un-
coordinated in the eyes of the tennis instructor? What have you
got to lose? You may never be noticed at all if you stay off the
courts; and just think how flattered the instructor will be at being
asked to teach you everything he or she knows about tennis.

A single woman friend, who travels frequently in her work,
used to bemoan the fact that "there I am in Cincinnati or San
Francisco for three or four days at a time with three or four lonely
evenings ahead of me." Most of her business dealings were with
married men and women who rushed home to the suburbs at the
close of business; so she usually wound up eating supper alone in
her hotel room.

Then she read an article in *Cosmopolitan,* advising women who
travel to make the most of their trips by asking the airline agent at
the gate to assign them a seat next to a good-looking man. She

thought she could never bear the risk of "appearing so aggressive," as she put it, until she found herself in line behind a beautiful and coolly collected woman who put that very question to the agent and was rewarded with a grin and a seat next to a famous actor.

Since then, my friend has tried it every time. She talks about the exciting conversations she's had with a variety of men in those "chance" meetings, who were equally delighted at the opportunity to offer her a cocktail and make her acquaintance. She still feels there's a risk involved in accepting a dinner date with a man about whom she knows nothing, but she's happily accepted dates in strange cities with fellow passengers who turned out to be residents of her own city, graduates of her own high school, friends of friends of hers, and sons of the women in her Aunt Ruby's bridge club!

"I suppose there's always a risk even if he turns out to be studying for the priesthood," she told me, with a wink. "But is it any riskier than taking a chance on a date with someone you meet at a singles bar?"

6. Overcome by Setbacks

There can be no denying the trauma that accompanies the death of a close friend, a parent or other relative. Death is so foreign to the single adult who is just emerging in life that he or she rarely knows how to deal with it. The loss of a job, being turned down for a date, the failure of an important relationship, even the most subtle possibility of rejection can also trigger depression and despair which, if unchecked, can result in emotional paralysis.

Setbacks are a part of life, one of the inherent risks in being born into a world over which you have less than complete control. But you do have the power to decide how you will react in times of crisis or under stress. If you "fall apart" at the first sign of adversity, it's because you choose to do so. You also have the option of choosing not to do so. Grief is to be expected at the loss of a loved one; a nervous breakdown is not.

The saintly virtue needed to counter the sin of being overcome by setbacks is adaptability.

By permitting oneself the freedom to fail, to express one's sorrow, and to experience the pain of disappointment or bereavement, one learns to draw on inner strengths which can be tapped again and again if need be.

A friend of mine was laid off by his employer and divorced by his wife in the same week. He confesses, "I didn't know how I would get through it. It seemed like my whole world was falling apart. But when I saw pity in the eyes of my friends, I took it as a challenge. I was *not* going to be crippled by those things as they expected me to."

Before long, he adds, "they were expressing admiration for my 'strength.' They were impressed with how quickly I landed a new job and began to seem like my 'old self.'

"Inwardly, I still had to deal with a lot of pain. But the experience gave me something else: confidence in my ability to take care of myself no matter what."

Claudia, a Chicago television producer who lost her job when the station where she worked changed hands, reports a similar phenomenon. "It took me six months to relocate, six months of having to make ends meet on ninety dollars per week in unemployment insurance after two years of living high on the hog in a $265-a-month apartment! In the beginning, I developed psychosomatic ailments every time I had to go to the unemployment office. But as time went by, I began to take a quiet sort of pride in my ability to survive. I ate a lot of tomato soup which, at nineteen cents a can, could be stretched out over two or more meals. I planned my automobile trips carefully so that I wouldn't have to travel back and forth across town twice in one day. I had very little money to spend on gasoline. And I moved into an apartment I could afford, learning to do without some of the luxuries I'd been used to."

The experience has taught her this: "I could do it all again if I had to without falling to pieces."

7. FAILURE TO TAKE GOD SERIOUSLY

Many singles claim to believe in God but adapt their personal conceptions of him to suit their own needs—calling on him in times of anguish, forgetting the power of prayer when things seem to be going well.

In doing so, they unwittingly reverse the roles, making "gods" of themselves and a servant of their Creator.

A sincere belief in God's influence at every stage of one's life leads to serious ongoing commitment and involvement in which one can experience personal satisfaction and peace of mind.

God is always faithful, available, and present in your life if you are ready to accept him.

I especially like the story related to me by a newspaperwoman from New York, who happened to be present at the birth of her cat's kittens. She stroked the cat's back as she went into labor and watched in awe as the cat performed the requisite operations in the precise order needed to insure the kittens' survival: clearing the kittens' mouths and nasal passages with a proficient flick of her tongue; cutting the umbilical cord with her teeth; washing and drying their matted fur—again with quick and highly efficient flicks of her tongue to prevent chilling and possible pneumonia; and then pulling them toward the nipples where they could immediately begin to draw vital nourishment and warmth. "She gave birth to five kittens, one by one, as I sat there in abject fascination, and it was the same procedure with each one. Where could she have learned all that? You have to believe in God and in a divine plan at a time like that when you consider that all of us were born just that way before we acquired the tools to pass on knowledge from one generation to the next. It makes me so secure and happy just to think of it that I could sing."

To remind oneself of God's hand in the most "trivial" of nature's triumphs and to think of him with gratitude in the good times are signs of a belief that can sustain a person through the worst of times.

Faith in God's reliability and resourcefulness can be measured in terms of a person's enthusiasm for living.

7. Single Power: Seven Lively Virtues

While much of my ministry has been geared to troubled singles, I couldn't help being impressed by their strengths as well. In many cases, singles troubled by loneliness exhibited a resiliency when confronted with setbacks that was nothing short of inspiring. Singles reduced to despondency in dead-end careers proved themselves time and again to be deeply sensitive, articulate, and compassionate human beings. The very willingness of these men and women to seek other resources when their own were found wanting was in itself an impressive source of strength.

For every deadly vice, there is a corresponding lively virtue, and for every lively virtue, thousands upon thousands of single men and women in whom it is vibrantly and inspiringly embodied.

Former president James Buchanan, Ralph Nader, Gore Vidal, Queen Elizabeth I, J. Edgar Hoover, Greta Garbo, Coco Chanel, Golda Meir, Tennessee Williams, Toulouse-Lautrec, Michelangelo, Gloria Steinem, Jean-Paul Sartre, Wilt Chamberlain, Dorothy Hammill, Vincent van Gogh, Joe Namath, David Brenner, Chicago mayor Michael J. Bilandic, California governor Edmund G. Brown, and "Miss Lillian" Carter are but a few of the unmarried or widowed past and present who embody so many virtues and whose achievements have been so remarkable as to inspire us all.

But one need not scan history books and newspaper headlines to find healthy, productive singles whose contributions to society render them exceptional, not only in comparison with other singles, but with the masses of us who fail for lack of trying.

Though it may come as a surprise to those who persist in viewing bachelorhood as an unhealthy state, the vast majority of singles *are* leading meaningful, productive lives. And while some single men and women seem to lead happier and more successful lives than others, there's a bit of the superior single in the least of them.

It takes a good deal of courage to cling to one's identity as a single person in a society whose institutions, most importantly whose churches, are geared to the married couple with a nuclear family. It takes a powerful dose of motivation to be entirely self-reliant in the midst of families whose burdens are eased by their interdependency on one another. Singles must try harder, persevere longer, cope with greater and more insidious forms of discrimination, exhibit more stoicism and patience, and establish more impressive credentials than their married peers in order to reap the same rewards and benefits. As a result, they quite often continue to persevere, to cope, and to struggle past the point where their married peers would rest on their laurels.

"Single power" is unfailingly impressive when viewed through unjaundiced eyes. It is a joy to behold the single who does not suffer from feelings of "incompleteness" for want of a mate, the single who takes concerted action to fill the voids in life without bemoaning the failure of others to do it for him or her, the single who is well-rounded, productive, and contented.

Interestingly, the number who are hostile to marriage is small indeed. Many look forward to finding that "special person" some day, viewing marriage as an enrichment to an already meaningful life, rather than as an escape hatch or a cure.

Seven lively virtues—*motivation, purposefulness, unselfishness, honesty, willingness to take risks, resiliency,* and *an abiding faith in God*—surface time and again in the lives of many singles. What follows is a description of how these qualities have enhanced the lives of eleven exceptional singles I have come to know and admire.

1. MOTIVATION

Sharon Preston is living proof of the adage, "Where there's a will, there's a way." Orphaned when she was six years old, she grew up with few advantages, initially in the care of an elderly grandmother who outlived Sharon's parents by only a few years. As the ward of family friends she was shuffled off to a series of Catholic boarding schools. But, looking back over a highly successful career as a New York-based reporter for a national news magazine, Sharon, now forty-four, believes that her strongest motivation came from the knowledge that she must take care of *herself.*

It was a motivation that never failed her at times when other singles, with parents to lean on, might have given up.

At the age of eighteen, lacking the funds to attend college, she found a job and entered night school. She eventually made job changes from receptionist to executive secretary until, through the want ads, she found a place in the field where she wanted to build a career. This time, it was working as a reporter's assistant for the magazine.

"Right from the start, I was doing almost the same work as the male reporters and getting the wages of a receptionist," she recalls. "But that didn't matter. What mattered was that I had the chance to build a career as a journalist." Having landed the job, she worked hard at it—often from 9:00 A.M. until 9:00 at night, skipping lunch hours, taking work home on weekends, reading up on city, state, and international affairs, digging up leads and developing potential news sources on her own time.

Her unerring sense of motivation led her to make certain sacrifices. For example, she admits, "I just haven't had the time to go out looking for eligible bachelors." She has a "very high regard for marriage and for women being helpmates to their husbands," she says. "But for me, marriage and sexual fulfillment must wait until I have developed my own interests and career." She has met a number of eligible men through her job, usually far more successful and well educated than the men other women find in singles bars. But she remains convinced that she couldn't have achieved professional success—her constant and abiding goal—if she had diverted her energies toward marriage.

"I know that most married people won't believe that a woman my age can be single and happy. I've been working twenty-six years. I started with no family to back me up, no money, and no credentials. But I have an inner peace that I don't believe a lot of married women have. And I am proud of it!"

Barry Sidel is a thirty-five-year-old Chicago bachelor earning in excess of fifty thousand dollars a year as executive vice-president of a highly respected Illinois mortgage company. He sees his role as being a "bridge" between the developer and the investor. It's an exciting profession to Barry, who has thrilled at each new challenge and has ascended rapidly because, as he would be the first to admit, he set a goal for himself and never lost sight of it.

In fact, Barry thrives on challenges and is almost continually setting new goals for himself. To rid himself of the anxieties and frustrations that almost inevitably accompany a studied rise to the top, he takes to the racquetball and tennis courts, where he is a vigorous competitor. He rarely misses the opportunity to play football in the Chicago Park District Tournament. His motivation as always is to win. "The more problems and responsibilities I have to deal with, the more physically active I become. Taking my frustrations out on that little ball serves as a tremendous mental release for me," he adds.

By setting a financial goal for himself, he was able to amass a sizeable enough nest egg to purchase a condominium on Astor Street on Chicago's affluent Near North Side. Now he declares with conviction, "I will be married within three years." Being single has been a definite advantage during his dogged pursuit of professional success, but marriage is an integral part of his next goal.

"I would like to buy a ranch with horses somewhere, perhaps in Arizona, and settle down. And I'm going to do it soon," he vows.

Somehow, there's no doubting that Barry can accomplish anything he sets his mind to.

Motivation isn't a quality that's born into a person but something that can be acquired when the alternative is painful enough. In the case of *Marie Calais,* it took ten years of marriage in Houston, Texas, to a man who drank heavily, spent money freely, and showed no interest in her or their two children, to generate the anger that spawned real motivation. "I looked in the mirror, and my face had the sadness of an old woman," says the thirty-eight-year-old divorcée, an exotic, olive-skinned beauty whose heritage is French and Yaqui Indian. "I looked at my drunken husband, and I told myself I was a bad mother to keep my sons in the same house with him. I looked at the marriages of my friends, and I didn't see any that were much better. So I decided that marriage was not for me."

She was twenty-seven (having married at seventeen) when she packed her sons and a few belongings on a bus and headed for St. Louis. "I didn't want a cent from my husband," she says of her haste in leaving. Her motivation: "to make it on my own."

She answered a newspaper ad for a dental assistant, no experience necessary, which paid a paltry fifty dollars a week; but it provided the experience she needed to change jobs several times, always in order to obtain more pay and more responsibility. She now manages an office for several dentists.

Her unflagging motivation has more than paid off. She earns more than several women she knows with college degrees. Her sons too are headed for responsible jobs with good incomes. One is attending a well-known art school on scholarship; the other is going to college nights and working days.

When her sons have completed their schooling, Marie plans to start college herself; she's already combing the community college catalogues. Why further her education when she's already doing so well? To increase her earnings, of course. It's all part of her next, exciting goal: to be able to finance vacations in Europe and South America.

2. PURPOSEFULNESS

Bill Cooper is chief of industrial supplies and equipment for all U.S. government offices in Chicago. He is black, single, and at the age of thirty, the youngest federal procurement branch office chief in the entire nation. Even as a youth, he stood out—attending college on a basketball scholarship, the only black among 5,500 whites on campus; living through seventeen months of front-line combat in Vietnam; embarking on a government career by taking a Civil Service examination and doing so well in subsequent training for entry-level positions that he was given his choice of government jobs. He chose procurement, a field offering responsibility as well as the opportunity to meet and work directly with many people.

"A lot of people expected me to fail. Some even wanted me to fail. I have had to work harder than most married white men who go home to family responsibilities," says Bill, explaining his decision to remain single, at least for the time being.

What has kept Bill plugging along when the going got rough was a sense of purpose he acquired as a young boy, the oldest of eight children born to hard-working, middle-class parents.

"I've always felt that I had to establish the standard for the rest of the children in the family. I'm proud that my father has had a long career as an electronics inspector. But I want my brothers and sisters to have me as well as my father as a model for success."

In that, Bill has already succeeded. His younger brothers and sisters look up with adoration at the big brother who owns his own two-story condominium furnished to his own taste and who is always greeted by name and served with alacrity in the restaurants where he likes to dine.

3. UNSELFISHNESS

Generous, compassionate, modest to a fault: That's *Dr. Olga Jonasson,* the forty-two-year-old chief of transplantation surgery and president of the medical staff at the Hospital of the University of Illinois.

Though she's received numerous professional honors, including an award as Outstanding Educator of America in 1971, she wryly credits some of her achievements to the fact that she's a woman at a time when many organizations and institutions are anxious to demonstrate that they are equal opportunity employers. Rather than dwell on her accomplishments during an interview, she insisted on setting forth her disappointments:

"Just this past week, I walked into one of Chicago's prestigious banks and inquired about a mortgage for the purchase of an old house I would like to buy and renovate. The loan officer didn't ask my name, how much money I make, or how long I've lived in the community. He didn't even give me an application. What I got was a sour-eyed, deprecating smile, which I took to mean 'You've got to be kidding, lady.'"

She also found herself less than welcome when, as a newcomer to Chicago, she began a painstaking search for a church home. In many churches, she found that "they had their own little cliques and they let you know it. When you visit, you are just that—a visitor." It took a long time, but when she finally found a church home, it was a tiny congregation in the heart of Chicago's Cabrini Green public housing project on Chicago's Near North Side. What did she find there? "The people are few in number, more real, more direct. They say what's on their mind and are more likely to discuss and accept grace than any others I've known."

Her life is her work, in itself a selfless, demanding, and time-consuming task; but she's always made time to assist in charity projects at her church. Currently serving as rummage sale chairman, she enthusiastically discusses some bargains to be found at her sales: "The best of the clothing sells for no more than a dollar, most items for a nickel."

One suspects that a substantial portion of the items sold for a fraction of their worth to those who can't afford to shop elsewhere came from Dr. Jonasson's own closets and from those of her friends. But she's not about to satisfy your curiosity. That would be boastful, and that wouldn't be Olga.

4. HONESTY

If there's one thing *Rodney Brown* of Milwaukee has learned to loathe in his sixty-six years of existence, it's hypocrisy. The sixth of seven children born to a Lutheran minister, he was taken to church every Sunday as a child simply "because everybody went to church in those days." But his father, who gave weekly sermons on love and devotion, seldom remembered Rodney's name and never remembered Rodney's birthday.

As a result, he grew up with a wary skepticism about the things that keep families together. As soon as he was old enough to leave home and live alone, he did so, working his way into a career as credit manager for a large textile manufacturer—an accomplishment in which Rodney, who never attended college, takes special pride.

In sixty-six years, Rodney considered marriage but decided against it in the end because although it was "the thing to do in those days" he honestly felt himself ill-suited to matrimony. He yearned for a more carefree life-style, hoping to travel, steer free of commitments, and earmark his savings for the purchase of coveted art objects. Today he is proud to say that he has traveled as far as England and India, amassing an imposing collection of priceless antiques and artifacts, has at times shared his home with financially strapped or emotionally troubled friends, and through it all has tried never to commit a hypocritical act.

Some may admire Brown, who is now retired, for the way in which he leads his life; others may have difficulty in understanding it. But to Rodney Brown, it is an immensely satisfying life, providing everything he ever hoped to accomplish.

"If I had married," he muses, "I hope I would have had the courage to make it a common-law marriage based on the spontaneous needs of both people."

But after sixty-six years of bachelorhood, he calls himself a contented man and wonders how many husbands can do the same.

5. The Willingness to Take Risks

JoAnne Brown majored in Spanish in college in preparation for a career in social work with Spanish-speaking people, "the sort of thing," she explains, "that women are encouraged to do." But after graduation, she found less demand for Spanish-speaking social workers than she had anticipated and settled for a job as a legal secretary instead. It wasn't a bad job, but she didn't view it as a "career." She was at her happiest at the end of her day when she could look forward to an evening out or at home with her friends. Sometimes, while in the shower or dressing for a date, she would turn on the radio and sing along. And that's about all the singing she'd be doing today, at the age of twenty-eight, if she hadn't been willing to take a risk.

"You know," her roommate had been telling her for some time, "you've got a great voice. You ought to develop your talent." And when JoAnne grew sufficiently bored with her typing and shorthand, she decided, Why not?

To overcome her initial fears, she began singing in church coffeehouses without pay and was sufficiently encouraged by the applause to sign up for guitar and voice lessons, financed by her earnings as a secretary. "If I didn't make it," she reasoned, "at least I could say I had really tried the one thing I wanted to do in my life." Happy with her decision, she also became happier in her job.

Finally, under the name Joey, she dared to face paying audiences during open-stage nights at a few well-known clubs.

"One night I was so nervous, I tripped and fell off the stage," she remembers. It was a humiliating experience, "and I knew I'd never sing again if I didn't face what had happened. So I came back the next night and did the whole performance again. Without falling."

Now she is earning additional income as a paid performer and is copyrighting songs she composed herself. The secretarial job remains a source of steady income which doesn't drain her of too much of the emotional energy she needs for practice and performances at night.

"It may be a frantic day," she admits. "Work until 4:30, then practice or a performance, then I usually have a friend over for dinner or some wine. But somehow it doesn't seem too frantic to me."

Satisfied with the results of the risk she has taken, JoAnne dares to think big. Above her bed hangs a huge, inflated plastic airplane—symbolic of her soaring ambitions. The rest of her five-room apartment is sparsely furnished.

"I want my voice to fill the room when I sing," she explains with a grin.

6. RESILIENCY

David Johnson is a twenty-six-year-old commercial airline pilot who has been flying since he was fourteen years old. Taught by his father, who was a World War II fighter pilot, David acquired his dad's love of maneuvering those big birds through the air. His ambition is to be a captain. And there seemed no stopping him in 1973 when he'd saved up enough money to realize a life-long ambition and purchased a used, single-engine Mooney aircraft for his personal use for $13,600.

But with the start of 1974 and the onset of the first nationwide fuel crisis, David's world seemed to cave in. Along with many other junior pilots, he was laid off.

"Naturally, I was disappointed and depressed. To lose your job is like losing your identity. I felt so insecure. All I wanted to do was hide.

"I was too proud to apply for unemployment compensation, but I was frightened. How would I pay my rent? How would I keep up the payments on my BankAmericard? The more I thought about it, the worse it seemed."

Luckily, David wasn't the sort to be disabled long by any set-back. After getting over the initial shock, he went job-hunting and landed a position in just two weeks as sales promotion manager for an aircraft corporation in Kerrville, Texas. It was a job he held for twenty-three months before being called back by his airline.

A less-resilient individual, one prone to follow the impulse to "hide" until being called back, would have invited financial ruin. David's ability to bounce back and draw on his inner reserves of confidence when the going got rough helped him avert disaster.

Jill Whitaker is a successful fashion model with apartments in Chicago and New York, a budding actress who has portrayed "Mrs. Average America" in a series of nationally televised food commercials, and who managed to land a bit with actors Robert Redford and Paul Newman in *The Sting*. By her own admission, it's an exciting existence. But life didn't look so glamorous a few short years ago when she came to Chicago from her native Three Oaks, Michigan, to look for a job as a home economics teacher.

Newly divorced, with just two suitcases full of clothes and a set of bedroom furniture to her name, she was badly in need of a job.

But there were no openings for home economics teachers anywhere in the Chicago area when Jill blew into town.

How she climbed from a state of near-destitution to an exciting and lucrative career in the entertainment world is a story, not of luck, but of resiliency: the ability to bounce back even stronger when misfortune strikes.

She went from one employment agency to another in search of any job that would pay a living wage. "But I couldn't even get a job as a teller in a bank that had several openings," says Jill, who was told she was "overqualified."

Finally, a sympathetic employment agency director took her on as a staff assistant, a job in which she was matching job candidates with better-paying jobs than the one she had and for which she continued to be "overqualified."

"It was hell. I did a lot of crying," she admits. "But at some point, I stopped crying and started thinking rationally." Evaluating her interests and assets, she decided that the world of fashion appealed to her, and she telephoned several modeling agencies whose names appeared in the Yellow Pages. "How does one go about becoming a model?" she asked. She'd need to have photographs taken, leave them with modeling and advertising agencies, and call every day to inquire about upcoming auditions for work, she learned.

"I had all the confidence of a newly released prisoner," she recalls. But eventually Jill got to a few auditions in which she learned a lot about make-up, hairstyles, and clothing by scrutinizing professional models who were landing the jobs.

Finally, she landed a few of her own—first as hostess at conventions; then to pose for newspapers and magazine ads; and finally to appear in fashion shows and TV commercials.

Her climb has been so dramatic that some acquaintances find it difficult to believe she has made it on her own, insinuating that she must have had to engage in promiscuity for assignments. Not Jill, who admits to a "social life that would seem dull to most singles—mostly staying home, reading, and listening to music."

She seldom indulges in alcoholic beverages. "How could I show up for a nine o'clock shooting if I had been out partying the night before?" she asks.

Jill's refusal to admit defeat when she was down and out got her where she is today—still on the way up!

Barbara B. Hirsch is a thirty-nine-year-old Chicago attorney to whom resilience is almost second nature. She might have written a book on the subject. As a matter of fact, she has written two thoughtful, perceptive, extremely informative books for divorcing and unmarried persons. They have undoubtedly helped many to avert or at least to prepare for misfortune before it strikes: *Divorce: What a Woman Needs to Know* and *Living Together: A Guide to the Law for Unmarried Couples.*

No financial setback is likely to incapacitate Barbara. She earns a substantial income and is scrupulous about managing and investing her earnings. Loneliness is something "I have never experienced," she says. Gaps in her life? "There aren't any. Being single is not like having a cavity that has to be filled. Being single is simply a description of my personal status."

If she ever marries, "and I am very much in favor of the idea of marriage between two people who love each other," she says, it will not be to fill any gap in her life but "because I would feel that my life could be even fuller and more productive in a married situation than in a single situation. Obviously, I have not met anyone who I think would make my life fuller, and so I am single."

The ultimate resiliency is to be prepared for any contingency, and if ever there was an individual who seemed in complete control of her destiny, that would be Barbara.

7. FAITH IN GOD

I can hear his music in my soul,
Praise the Lord, Praise the Lord!

And it sings in my heart like a hot and blazing coal,
Praise the Lord, Praise the Lord!
Through the day, through the night,
In the darkness, in the light,
Each condition of my life comes from his hand;
In the clouds, underground,
On the sea, on the land,
Praise the Lord, Praise the Lord!

The bachelor who composed that stirring hymn is also the award-winning composer of the scores for a whole slew of off-Broadway productions and the man who directed *Home Movies* in 1964, *Gorilla Queen* in 1966, *In Circles* in 1968, *Peace* and *Promenade* in 1969, *Wanted* and *Joan* in 1972 and *The Faggot* in 1973. He is also a television producer, preacher, and performer who has lectured at universities, colleges, and seminaries throughout the country. He has appeared on the "Tonight Show," the "Today Show," and the "Mike Douglas Show."

The almost incredibly talented and versatile individual is Al Carmines, pastor of Judson Memorial Church in New York City. His unquestioning faith is eloquently expressed in the hymns written for and sung each Sunday morning by the congregation of his church.

Carmines's faith is an all-encompassing, shout-it-from-the-rooftops kind of faith; his philosophy of life is based on truthfulness. "Follow the truth, and religion will catch up with you," Carmines maintains, insisting that the challenge of the single life is to take the moment seriously, to live in the "now" where you actually are.

Too often, says Carmines, singles buy into the myth that you're "on your way," in the process of preparing for the future, but not really an adult until you're married.

Carmines's strength as a single adult and his faith are so abiding that he seems to energize all who are touched by his words, his music, and most particularly his sermons that are lively, humorous, and geared to a modern audience. This excerpt is from a sermon in defense of the Pharisees:

Our image of Pharisees is of a bunch of money-grubbing hypocrites rushing around the streets looking for someone to crucify. Nothing could be further from the truth about most of the Pharisees. They were for the most part modest, faithful, charitable, kind people. They would rank well in the religious liberal avant garde of our own day.

But they did believe one thing that put them in immediate conflict with Jesus, and that was, that religion was somehow special in a way that changed your status before God. And so when Jesus said, "Look boys, the whores and the loan sharks will get into heaven before you," it was disturbing. But that's what He did say . . .

In the same sermon, Carmines applauded Billy Graham for his response to a woman who confessed difficulty in believing that a "just" God would accept the thief on the cross who repented at the last minute as readily as a saintly person. "I thought Dr. Graham handled the question well. He told her not to worry so much about the thief on the cross and concentrate a little more on herself," Carmines told the congregation.

Carmines's strength and confidence are drawn in large measure from his expansive faith in which, as the concluding stanza of that hymn points out:

Praising God is the privilege of all
Black and white, straight and gay,
Old and young, short and tall;
Praise the Lord, Praise the Lord,
Praise the Lord!

8. The Challenge

There is little doubt that the singles phenomenon is putting pressure on the church. The problem is that this pressure has resulted in a closing of ranks and doors rather than in a reaching out to enfold strays within the flock. The mystery is why the church does not recognize and accept the challenge of singles as emanating from God.

From the beginning of Christianity, God has utilized the challenge of external pressure to push, shove, and move his people out into the world "that the world may believe." At the ascension of Jesus, for example, the angels said, "Men of Galilee, why do you stand there looking up at the sky?" (Acts 1:11, TEV). A humorous way to say: Move!

The persecution of the early church was the obvious external pressure that forced Christians to scatter throughout the world.

Today too the Lord is utilizing external pressures to push, shove, and move Christians out into the world "that the world may believe." In my observation, God has visited four influential external pressures on American churches in our times.

1. *The growth of vast metropolitan urban centers,* in which highrise, multifamily dwellings have had to be developed to accommodate steadily increasing numbers of people on constantly diminishing acres of land, leading to increasingly impersonal life-styles.

2. *The need for communication between the urban centers,* in which American workers and their families have become increasingly mobile.

3. *The rapid industrialization of our nation,* with its emphasis on the production of increasingly efficient, time-saving, and labor-saving devices, leading us into an increasingly leisure-oriented life-style.

4. *A postwar population "explosion," already exerting a worrisome drain on our natural resources,* in which contraception is easily practiced, abortion is legalized, and nearly fifty million American adults remain unmarried.

Together, these four factors have forced twentieth-century Christians to examine more seriously the effectiveness of their mission and the very meaning of their existence in America.

Time's pendulum is swinging away from the nuclear, single-family dwelling that constituted the norm a scant generation ago. Apartment living is the norm for more and more people. And with good reason. As a study issued by the Department of Housing and Urban Development and former President Ford's Council on Environmental Quality pointed out during the last administration, "The traditional single-family home is the most expensive to build and inefficient to operate."

The multifamily dwelling also turns out to be ecologically sounder, generating on the average "about 45 percent less air pollution, less water pollution, and up to some 44 percent less energy consumption" than the single-family home, according to the report.

If the trend continues, and there's been no indication that it won't, more than half of all Americans will be living in apartment-type communities by the year 2000.

The potential impact of the stability of the church is impossible to assess with any certainty, but it's bound to be substantial.

As for those already dwelling in apartments, condominiums, mobile homes, and planned communities, Larry McSwain, of the

Southern Baptist Convention's Home Mission Board, declared flatly: "Few churches are attempting any specialized ministry to this segment for our population."[17] This is the case despite the fact that, as Alvin Toffler wrote in *Future Shock,* one of the greatest crises for a human being is changing his or her place of residence.

According to McSwain's findings:

1. The average American moves fourteen times in his or her lifetime compared to eight moves in Great Britain and five changes of address in the lifetime of the average citizen of Japan.
2. One out of every five persons in America changes addresses every year.
3. The telephone disconnect rate now averages 25 percent per year.

How could the church reach and minister to the needs of people on the move? How can the church be a blessing to those experiencing the great crisis of changing addresses? It is necessary that they be recognized as needy recipients of God's message.

Still another external pressure confronting the church today is society's leisure-oriented life-style. According to *U.S. News & World Report,* Americans spend over $146 billion a year on leisure goods. The money Americans are now spending on spare-time activities exceeds national defense costs. Estimates are that the dollar volume of leisure-time expenditures will more than double during the decade of the 70's.

How can the church compete for those dollars against Superbowl Sunday, getaway weekends, and the manufacturers of ski boots and sailboats?

In the midst of all this, the challenge presented by the emergence of a vast, skeptical singles population constitutes a

[17] Larry McSwain, "The Challenges of Ministry with Persons in Multi-family Housing" (paper read at Listening Dialogue Conference on Apartment Ministry, Atlanta, Georgia, August 12, 1975).

genuine search for meaning and purpose. As Father Patrick H. O'Neill, representative for Campus and Young Adult Ministry and editor of *National Young Adult Reporter*, points out:

> By far the strongest cry for meaning comes from young adults, age 18–35, who in large numbers, are not only disenfranchised from the traditional structures, standards and messages of society but, more tragically, from the Church itself. In some cases, that alienation manifests itself in contempt.
>
> However, the young adults who have left the institution because of what they identify as sexism, racism, cowardice and hypocrisy, continue to hunger, most often in vain, for a community of love, hope, and peace, as promised in the message of Jesus.[18]

Single Americans are the most vulnerable to the external pressures threatening us all. They move most frequently, typically live in an apartment, and more actively pursue a leisure-oriented life-style than their married counterparts.

Confronted by these powerful external pressures, will the church rise to meet the challenge? Or will it continue to bend the gospel to its own self-serving interests, only utilizing portions which glorify the traditional nuclear-family life-style?

Will the lay leadership continue to operate as a closed corporation, preoccupied with preserving the status quo? Or will it embrace the passion of God's love and begin dealing meaningfully with the entire spectrum of the human condition as Jesus did when he preached good news to the poor and healed the brokenhearted?

The real challenge facing the church today is to *wake up!* We need to listen to God's Word, to hear and believe what God is trying to communicate. The message is there. God is there. He cares about people. He put his life on the life for all people.

God does not withdraw from sinners, and we are all sinners.

[18]Fr. Patrick H. O'Neill (ed.), *National Young Adult Reporter* I, 1 (Autumn 1976): 5.

God does not offer himself contingent upon any conditions or requirements.

John said, "Herein is love, not that we loved God, but that he loved us, and sent his Son to be the propitiation for our sins. Beloved, if God so loved us, we ought also to love one another" (1 John 4:10, 11).

Isaiah said, "He is despised and rejected of men; a man of sorrows, and acquainted with grief: and we hid as it were our faces from him; he was despised, and we esteemed him not. Surely he hath borne our griefs, and carried our sorrows: yet we did esteem him stricken, smitten of God, and afflicted. But he was wounded for our transgressions, he was bruised for our iniquities: the chastisement of our peace was upon him; and with his stripes we are healed. All we like sheep have gone astray; we have turned every one to his own way; and the Lord hath laid on him the iniquity of us all" (Isa. 53:3–6).

Paul said, "For when we were yet without strength, in due time Christ died for the ungodly. For scarcely for a righteous man will one die: yet peradventure for a good man some would even dare to die. But God commendeth his love toward us, in that, while we were yet sinners, Christ died for us" (Rom. 5:6–8).

Luke said, "Be it known unto you therefore, men and brethren, that through this man is preached unto you the forgiveness of sins: And by him all that believe are justified from all things, from which ye could not be justified by the law of Moses" (Acts 13:38, 39).

God is good! He cares about people. He knows what people need. "Seventy times seven" we are forgiven. "As far as the East is from the West" our sins have been removed. "Though our sins be as scarlet, they shall be as white as snow: though they be red like crimson, they shall be as wool" we are assured.

The message we should be getting is about God's *faithfulness, love, mercy, endurance,* and *victory over sin.*

The message is that we have all been made recipients of his

goodness. As the Apostle Paul said, "by grace . . . you have been saved, through faith; not by anything of your own, but by a gift from God; not by anything that you have done, so that nobody can claim the credit. We are God's work of art, created in Christ Jesus to live the good life as from the beginning he had meant us to live it" (Eph. 2:8–10, JB).

The challenge to the church is to be alive with the love of God in our hearts, celebrating life. God's message was not confined to the nuclear family. How can anyone dare to obscure or put conditions on the goodness of God? Does anyone but God have a right to make changes, add rules or requirements to his message? God's love is not subject to interpretation, qualification, or restriction; it is not intended to be stored for occasional selective use.

God's love for people must not be permitted to give way in a church council's justification of a particular style for living.

On the contrary, the church must embrace the commandment first given through Moses, "Love thy neighbour as thyself" (Lev. 19:18), and restated by Christ, "A new commandment I give unto you, That ye love one another" (John 13:34). A common weakness among church people is a failure to love themselves. Perhaps this stems from their inability to perceive correctly the love of God.

In his Letter to the Colossians, Paul wrote:

> You are the people of God; he loved you and chose you for his own. So then, you must put on compassion, kindness, humility, gentleness, and patience. Be helpful to one another, and forgive one another, whenever any of you has a complaint against someone else. You must forgive each other in the same way that the Lord has forgiven you. And to all these add love, which binds all things together in perfect unity. The peace that Christ gives is to be the judge in your hearts; for to this peace God has called you together in the one body. And be thankful. Christ's message, in all its richness, must live in your hearts (Col. 3:12–17, TEV).

The challenge to churches is to wake up and listen to God's

message. A radical revision in church life is called for, incorporating a sincere acceptance of the gospel in which divergent nationalities, tongues, and life-styles are drawn together and enfolded in the all-encompassing love of God, a forgiving love that does not insist on uniformity or conformity.

Pluralism is God's gift to humankind. It should be celebrated.

Church councils must be reminded that the value or attractiveness of their buildings and grounds, the size of their membership rolls, and the number of sopranos in the choir loft are secondary, minor considerations.

The emergence of single adults as viable, contributing members of church and society should be accepted, encouraged, and celebrated—by their co-worshipers. The model, the nuclear family, need not crumble when people learn to deal more openly and honestly with one another.

When the message of Christ is alive and living in their hearts, church leaders and churchgoers will cease to fear one another, and the church will be healthier and more integral a part of their lives than it has ever been.

People have always related better to one another in associations built on foundations of mutual tolerance and trust. Good relationships need "working at."

Too many people seek church weddings in the assumption that a religious ceremony is all it takes to "make" a marriage. Then they divorce and explain resignedly that things "just didn't work out."

Christ's message is aimed at removing barriers—such as the "stigma" of divorce and the "failures" of some singles to live as their elders might wish. Divorced people, particularly, need to be given the support to deal with the trauma, learn from their mistakes, and pick up the pieces of their splintered lives.

The church has the means and the power to become the healer of the multitude of problems it has been accused of creating. The message of Christ calls for love of God and of one another, compassion, kindness, humility, gentleness, and patience. This was the message in the beginning, and it remains our most cherished goal to the end. Why have we let ourselves grow so indifferent to one another? What can be done to shorten the distances between us?

Television stations take corrective action whenever their ratings drop. The church's failure to secure better ratings among single adults also points to a need for drastic corrective action. It should encourage relationships between people of different lifestyles and generations to work out their tensions and difficulties. What then would we have to look forward to? Happier homes, better marriages, and a more integrated community, for starters, a world in which we can move toward loving acceptance of one another.

Dr. Paul Tournier, a Swiss doctor, maintains that "no one can develop freely in this world and find a full life without feeling understood by at least one person. . . .

"Listen to all the conversation of our world, between nations as well as those between couples. They are, for the most part, dialogues of the deaf."[19]

The basic human need—to be really listened to, to be taken seriously, to be understood—*can* by fulfilled by the church.

When the church with the rich message of God in its heart captures this feeling of genuine human warmth and concern for others, it will begin echoing the concern, warmth, and passion of God. The results would be exciting, ideal church communities of marrieds and singles: confessing individually and together; forgiving one another as God has forgiven them; accepting themselves and others in sharing new and unique fellowships; growing

---

[19] Paul Tournier, *To Understand Each Other* (Richmond, Virginia: John Knox Press, 1967), p. 29ff.

in grace and understanding as they help one another face their problems and set new goals; preaching the Word of God and administering the sacraments as the source of direction and power for life; joining together financially to support the maintenance of this fellowship according to their means; and sincerely willing to accept diversity as one of God's loveliest gifts.

Here are some of the yearnings of ordinary churchgoers:

Rayna Raulerson, a Fort Lauderdale, Florida, newspaperwoman, described her concept of an ideal church in a conversation with me:

"My ideal church would not be clogged up with rules and so much formality. I think churches are too formal. It's pretty sad when people think they can't go to church because they don't feel they have the right clothes to wear. I also think the church is more afraid than it need be of change. Churches have to be open and warm. Too often, they are cold and sterile. Ministers should be accessible. Someone should be on hand to help you any time of the day, not just by appointment. Instead of addressing the women's clubs and the Kiwanis, ministers should be available to people who need help. I think it's horrible for a church to be closed and locked ever. My ideal church would have a congregation of people who were willing to help one another and not just say that they're Christian and love their fellow man. They would show it. There doesn't need to be a vacuum in society for do-gooders. You could do good through the church."

An active, churchgoing, sixty-two-year-old mother of five daughters in a mid-western city wishes that the church would take a more active role in disseminating information about and guidance concerning such important human matters as love, sex, marriage, dating, and family relationships.

"My oldest daughter," she said, "is probably still a virgin. She's forty-two years old. We were too darn protective. We thought we were doing the right thing. Now my youngest, who's just about to graduate from college, is having her second abortion. I wish the church would help. I mean really help! Simply telling them to get married is not the solution. What I want them to do is find real happiness and love if that's still possible. That's what we ought to be talking about. I know I would be willing to sit on a church panel and share my feelings. It seems to me that if we work together we could make some real discoveries and provide the help people are looking for."

Marrieds and singles sharing with one another the struggles, joys, aspirations, and rich diversity of their lives *can* happen. In my opinion, the church is the best possible arena in which it can be made to happen.

The challenge now is to move from an awareness of what the Gospel says to a clear understanding of what it means, in terms of the world in which we're now living.

First and foremost, it means that God's message is for *all* people. "Go ye into all the world, and preach the gospel to every creature" (Mark 16:15) is our Lord's command to his apostles. All four New Testament Gospel writers record this command of Jesus, and few Christians today would argue that the church should be in mission. Christians, however, differ from time to time as to how and when or even to what extent the church should do mission work. Nevertheless, it is important to realize the serious desire God has for Christians—his followers—to be about his business in today's world.

Today's church can overcome any obstacle if it takes to heart the example of the early Christians, driven from their comfortable nests. For them, it was move out or be fed to the lions.

The same is true today. The church must move out of its comfortable nest and into the high-rise, highly mobile, often alienated and otherwise-occupied world of the never-married, divorced, sexually liberated and bereaved, if it is to remain the church God intended.

The church must move out beyond the white picket fences of

suburbia or be crippled by monotony, inflexibility, insensitivity, lack of vision, and total misunderstanding of God's great "Go ye." Otherwise, a marked deficiency of faith will be the bench mark for the twentieth-century Christian church in America.

God utilizes external pressures in today's society as effectively as he did with the early church. His message, and it bears repeating, is that *all* are to be recipients of his messages. He wants his church to be out in the world demonstrating the love of God.

The understanding of this clear imperative of Jesus along with the proper concern about the external pressures confronting the church today will enable the church to function responsibly in the future.

Furthermore, the church must *not* depend on evangelism for its institutional survival but rather go about its evangelistic pursuits in the unselfish spirit expressed by Harold R. Cook, missionary at the Orinoco River Mission in Venezuela:

. . . the attitude of the missionary should not be that of one who goes to others to get anything, whether followers, or merit, or rewards, or praise, or appreciation. It should be that of one who gives, who gives because he must give, who learned to give from the One who "so loved the world that he gave his only begotten son."[20]

Christ showed us how. He set the pattern for Christians of all generations. He said his mission was to serve others: "Whosoever will be great among you, shall be your minister: And whosoever of you will be the chiefest, shall be servant of all. For even the Son of man came not to be ministered unto, but to minister, and to give his life a ransom for many" (Mark 10:43–45).

At the most crucial time of our Lord's life, mission work occupied his mind. Moments before his capture by the soldiers in the Garden of Gethsemane, he expressed his most urgent and sincere wishes: "I pray not that thou shouldest take them out of the

[20] Harold R. Cook, *Missionary Life and Work* (Chicago: Moody Press, 1964), p. 166.

world, but that thou shouldest keep them from evil. . . . As thou has sent me into the world, even so have I also sent them into the world" (John 17:15, 18).

Our Lord's prayer is that we who believe should carry his word out into the world. Why does Jesus want his followers to carry his word out into the world? "That they all may be one; . . . that the world may believe that thou hast sent me. . . . and that the world may know that thou has sent me, and hast loved them, as thou hast loved me" (John 17:21–23).

The challenge of the church, therefore, is to listen to the Gospel, live the Gospel, and be responsive to the command of Christ by continually being in mission to all people in a changing world. The church must not oppose but rather join the struggle and search of singles in their quest for sincere forms of fellowship.

The door to the church is Janus-faced. On one side, it must be unlocked and opened by the church itself. On the other, it must be knocked upon and entered by the singles. A welcome mat is a sad gesture if no one ever comes to call. If singles are to receive God into their hearts, the challenge is theirs as well. They must be willing to knock on the door of the church and insist on their rightful place among the congregation.

They cannot afford the luxury of sitting back and waiting for the church to minister to their needs. It's up to singles to make those needs urgently and unequivocally understood.

In spite of the discrimination, hostility, or pressure they may encounter as they begin to come forward, come forward they must—to hear and assist in disseminating God's Word. Singles can rise above these dehumanizing encounters by listening and responding to the Gospel.

The disaffected single's value will be to doggedly remind the church that it exists, not to perpetuate itself, but to serve all people within and beyond its reach and to reevaluate its methods when it falls short of that imperative.

The church must realize its shortcomings, wasteful practices, and injustices whenever and wherever they occur; it must continually reexamine, confess, and renew itself as it would have its parishioners do so that what the church implies on Sunday morning applies during the rest of the week.

To be sure, righteous, dogmatic ministers will preach fiery, colorful sermons without touching the human condition; but even they can be patiently, lovingly, and persistently confronted on a one-to-one basis.

The church must also come to understand how unappealing its preoccupation with money is to the struggling young adult. The questions he or she poses are not expressions of unfaithfulness but a challenge of faith—an opportunity in which faith can be made even stronger.

Singles have an obligation to explain why they feel alienated, uncommitted, and disturbed in the church as it's now constructed. Singles need to discuss with their married churchgoing counterparts how serious an impact the turbulent events of the past years have had on their lives. Within the past fifteen years a man has walked on the moon, three national leaders have been assassinated, and black ghettos in Watts and Chicago have burned. We have witnessed innumerable student protests, a widespread sexual revolution, the advent of the feminist movement, the forced resignation of a sitting president, a growing skepticism about the sincerity and motives of institutions generally, an all-time high divorce rate, louder cries from the poor and hungry, unstemmed exploitation and pollution of our national resources in the name of profit, a nationwide energy crisis, and the emergence of consumer advocates—such as Ralph Nader—as folk heroes.

It's up to single persons to share their idealism and sense of urgency with the church establishment. Together, they have an opportunity to turn this planet around, but it will require a mutual willingness to share their concern openly, honestly, and unreservedly with one another.

When that happens, the sincerity of the heart and spirit that the prophet Isaiah called for as true religion can be realized:

> Take your wrongdoing out of my sight.
> Cease to do evil.
> Learn to do good,
> search for justice,
> help the oppressed,
> be just to the orphan,
> plead for the widow (Isa. 1:16–17, JB).

9. Affirmative Action: What the Church Can Do?

Church people, individually and together, can do a lot to narrow the gaps that exist between singles and the church. A voice within the power structure of the church or parish council, a meeting place for their gatherings, and greater access to the pastor are some of the things asked for by single men and women. But behind any attempt to facilitate communication between the establishment church and alienated single adults, the church must exhibit a *sincere* willingness to accept singles on their own terms. To offer singles a voice in matters of policy and planning, provided they don't "rock the boat," is a sham that any unwitting "token" member will find repugnant, causing more harm than good in the long run.

The importance of dealing forthrightly and in a nonthreatening manner with single adults, in or out of the church setting, can not be overemphasized. To do otherwise is to discount their ability to think and conduct themselves as effectively as their married peers and can only drive them farther away.

Here are some things a progressive pastor and congregation can do immediately to facilitate the return of alienated single adults:

1. REQUIRE THAT AT LEAST ONE-THIRD OF YOUR CHURCH COUNCIL OR GOVERNING BOARD BE SINGLE MEN AND WOMEN.

This figure represents the approximate percentage of singles in the community-at-large. The same principle should be applied with regard to women and other minority members.

The axiom "Physician, heal thyself" applies here. There is no better place to start than right at home with a wholesale reevaluation and revision of the existing power structure of the church. When unmarried and divorced adults have a voice in establishing church policies and disbursement priorities, they will have less cause for complaint about how their personal contributions are spent. When they are permitted to take part in creating and directing programs of their choosing, they will be more apt to support them as participants.

Married board or council members are also likely to benefit from their increased exposure to intelligent, creative, concerned single adults.

The push for sincere acceptance of the single parishioner must originate within and enjoy the strong, continued support of the existing power structure if any other attempts to open up lines of communication are to have value.

2. REQUIRE THAT THE SECOND PASTOR BE SINGLE AND BE GIVEN A SALARY, BENEFITS, AND RESPONSIBILITIES MATCHING THE FIRST MINISTER'S.

The opportunity to hire a second pastor is commonly regarded as an opportunity to provide "assistance" to the first or senior pastor. All too often, perhaps unwittingly, church councils permit too wide a gap to exist between their pastors in age, salary, and responsibilities. In cases like these, the senior pastor is apt to control and dominate in practically every matter of church policy or procedure, and the "junior" pastor allows himself or herself to be cowed into obeisance out of respect for the "elder."

Nothing so neatly perpetuates the myth that the young, single adult is somehow "inferior," regardless of qualifications and training. The subtle distinctions are perfectly discernible to church members, who will continue to regard the unmarried minister as "less worthy" until the church takes steps to make him or her an equal partner in a *dual* ministry.

It goes without saying that any pastor considered for such a role should be qualified to deal with all congregants, regardless of their age, sex, or marital status; but the church fathers may be pleasantly surprised to discover how excellent a job our seminaries are doing these days in preparing young clerics to cope with problems that were rarely discussed a few decades ago.

3. ESTABLISH THAT A PASTOR'S LENGTH OF SERVICE TO THE CONGREGATION IS NOT TO EXCEED TWELVE YEARS.

It's difficult for pastors who have served the parish for a long time and expect to remain in control for the remainder of their lifetime to resist the temptation to rest on past laurels. As complacency sets in, so does a tendency to view any innovation through lenses distorted by the imperative of "tradition." Out of what many believe to be "respect for the old boy," parishioners are loath to challenge his assertions. In short, there is no pressure on pastor or flock to adapt to changes in the world about them.

As a result, the most loving thing a congregation can do, for its pastor and the church membership at large, is to establish a limit to the length of service at the time of hiring. It will also serve as a needed challenge to the pastor to place the desire for tenure in proper perspective to the continuing relevance of ministry in a rapidly changing world.

The purpose in establishing such a requirement is respect and not disrespect, challenge and not stagnation. The pastor who has reached the twelve-year point in the parish will know the love and gratitude of those he or she will be leaving and will be challenged to renew commitment among a different set of people.

4. SPONSOR HUMAN SEXUALITY WORKSHOPS FOR SINGLES, LED BY DOCTORS, PSYCHIATRISTS, AND PASTORS.

Such workshops exist elsewhere—in schools, hospitals, family planning clinics, private therapy groups, and the like—but in most cases, something is sadly lacking in all such attempts to "enlighten" men and women about the problems and potentials of their bodies, namely, a loving, moral, inspirational framework.

As a result, sexually liberated people are heard to mutter among themselves, "I'm free and you're free, so why aren't we happy?" Sexual freedom usually means sexual irresponsibility; and sexual enslavement means perpetual unhappiness. When an atmosphere of honesty, trust, and warmth is lacking, these problems are rarely given the attention they deserve, in or out of the church setting.

Sexuality workshops, if they are competently and compassionately conducted, can be an effective means of dealing with an important but delicate matter. I cannot envision a more appropriate setting than the church itself—a fellowship of people who care about one another.[21]

5. ESTABLISH AN ALTERNATIVE WORSHIP SERVICE FOR THOSE UNWILLING OR UNABLE TO ATTEND THE REGULAR SUNDAY MORNING SERVICE.

The sharp decline in attendance at Sunday morning services during the past couple of decades has too often been viewed as an overt rebellion against the church itself in a society corrupted by evil. This is not necessarily the case. In fact, churches that have experimented with additional or alternative services at other times of the day or on other days of the week have been rewarded with crowds surpassing their wildest expectations.

[21]*For further information:* Program of Human Sexuality, University of Minnesota, School of Medicine, 2630 University Avenue S.E., Minneapolis, Minnesota 55414 (612) 376–7520; Human Sexuality Program, Northwestern University Medical School, Department of Psychiatry, c/o Jane Barclay Mandel, 303 E. Chicago Avenue, Chicago, Illinois 60611 (312) 649–8050.

The need to worship is not on the decline; it's a matter of drastically altered life-styles. The majority of Americans no longer live to work; they work to live. People can scarcely be blamed for seeking a day of rest if Sunday is the only morning when a worker can sleep past 9 A.M. without being docked by his employer or if the weekend is the only opportunity for working people and their families to plan joint outings.

Pastors who exhort their congregations, as an Atlanta minister does at every opportunity, not to "bother" them with requests for shorter services, later services, or more entertaining services and who condemn them for their unwillingness to "make sacrifices" are exercising judgmental options not in keeping with the spirit of the gospel.

It's difficult to prescribe the ideal time and setting for an alternative worship service; the circumstances will vary from one community to another. A church located in a large manufacturing community in which thousands of workers are regularly required to work evening or weekend shifts may wish to stagger two or more services over a period of days. Many Catholic churches have had success with Saturday or Sunday evening services. Other denominations have instituted Wednesday evening services which have become particularly popular among younger members of the congregation. Some singles prefer a traditional Sunday service, "But why not an hour or two later, maybe starting at noon?" in the words of one Chicago bachelor.

The alternative service can also provide an opportunity for less formal modes of worship on an experimental basis, prior to introduction into the regular service.

6. INVITE SINGLES GROUPS TO UTILIZE CHURCH FACILITIES WITHOUT FINANCIAL CHARGE.

Organizations of single people in search of fellowship and peer support, ranging from ski clubs to volleyball teams to Parents Without Partners, have sprung up all over the nation. Already organized, having their own membership lists and schedule of programs, but usually operating on a limited financial base, they only have one need in common: a facility in which to get together and conduct their meetings. Churches that open their doors to such groups render a valuable service to singles and at the same time provide themselves an opportunity to open up lines of communication that might not otherwise exist. Singles permitted to use church facilities frequently expressed the desire to make reciprocal gestures, out of gratitude to the church. Oftentimes, they are more apt to "try" the Sunday service in the church that has been host to their own Thursday-night club than the seemingly impregnable church around the corner. (Of course, the church around the corner may be just as eager to have them on Sunday morning but has not gone out of its way to demonstrate that eagerness.)

7. CONSTRUCT OR ESTABLISH A CASUAL, COMFORTABLE, AND GRACIOUS MEETING CENTER WHERE SINGLES (AND OTHER) GROUPS CAN GATHER AND EXCHANGE IDEAS.

Given a choice between a homelike meeting place with plush couches, a crackling hearth fire, and the aroma of freshly brewed coffee wafting in from a nearby kitchen or a stark, sterile institutional hall with steel folding chairs and cracked plaster, singles are no different from the rest of us: They'll opt for the setting in which they can relax in comfort.

Any doubts on that were settled for me when my Transactional Analysis group voted unanimously to meet in my apartment rather than in the sparsely furnished meeting room at our disposal. It's impossible to minimize the necessity for a commodious, if not luxurious, meeting center. The color of the walls, the use of indoor plants and soft lighting, and a conversation-pit seating arrangement can all be used to produce a feeling of intimacy, warmth, and belonging.

The establishment of a comfortable meeting place ought not be regarded as an extravagance. A simple, little corner in the basement is rarely adequate for anything other than storage. Churches need to place the development of convivial lounges and meeting rooms among their top priorities if they sincerely want their members to feel "at home" in the facilities.

8. DEMONSTRATE YOUR AWARENESS OF THE VARIOUS FORMS OF DISCRIMINATION TO WHICH SINGLE ADULTS ARE SUBJECTED.

There's no getting around the fact that singles have to pay higher automobile and health insurance premiums and more federal income tax. They're unable to get tax credit for the portion of their rental payments that is used to pay property taxes—a deduction enjoyed by the average American homeowner. Singles also find it difficult to obtain loans and are frequently passed over for promotion by their employers in favor of married co-workers who are presumed to be "more stable." The last thing they want of a church, in which they are generally excluded from the family-oriented programs and activities, is a further lack of compassion for the real forms of discrimination to which they are continually subjected on the outside.

9. DO NOT VIEW THE NEEDS OF DIVORCED PARISHIONERS AS MATTERS OF LOW PRIORITY.

A divorce is not a perversion but a forthright and honest approach to dealing with a shattered relationship. Each partner is given an opportunity to start over; yet some unbending churchmen and women persist in viewing the unhappy spouse who drinks himself into a stupor as the "more Christian." The stigma attached to the divorced person in the mind of the uncharitable, dispassionate pastor and flock is the more serious problem. The truly concerned pastor has an obligation to do everything in his or her power to provide an atmosphere of acceptance and support for the man or woman going through one of the most traumatic of life's crises. The number of divorced people in the congregation should not determine whether or not to deal with the subject in sermons, discussion groups, and workshops. It's the attitudes of those not going through marital crises that must be changed, however long it takes.

10. VIEW THE NEVER-MARRIED, THE DIVORCED, AND THE WIDOWED AS COMPLETE INDIVIDUALS.

At birth a human being is completely formed and endowed with all the equipment he or she needs to lead a useful and productive life. None of us are "born" husbands and wives; nor can we be said to be incomplete when a spouse is lost through death or divorce. God became flesh and dwelt among us in the person of a bachelor, Jesus Christ. Who could be more complete than he?

11. SPONSOR DISCUSSION GROUPS AND DIALOGUES IN WHICH SINGLES AND MARRIEDS CAN BEGIN TO KNOW, TRUST, AND LEARN FROM ONE ANOTHER.

Once friendships are established, marital status is rarely a deterrent to participation. Until about a year ago, I routinely scheduled rap sessions and wine and cheese parties for singles. I was surprised to be told by a newlywed, who had attended frequently "Don't count me out just because I'm married." With a jolt, I realized that I had been discriminating against newly married people who could derive as much benefit from these activities as single persons. I no longer exclude the marrieds and am happy to report that these sessions are going better than ever.

12. LET SINGLES SPEAK FOR THEMSELVES.

You may think you know another's needs better than he or she does, but this is rarely the case. To deny a single adult the right to make his or her opinion known is to seriously jeopardize his or her sense of personal integrity and worth. More important, married churchgoers can benefit from the opportunity to hear firsthand what singles are all about. Given the respect and accorded dignity, singles are apt to respond accordingly: with dignity, respect, and gratitude.

13. STOP FEELING SORRY FOR SINGLES.

Not to do so is to perpetuate the myth that the unmarried adult is somehow inferior. The single adult doesn't want your sympathy. All he or she asks is your acceptance.

14. LEAD YOUR FELLOW CHURCHMEN TO ACKNOWLEDGE THE CONTRIBUTIONS MANY SINGLES ARE MAKING IN SOCIETY, AND OPENLY APPLAUD THOSE WHO EXCEL.

Unmarried adults are vital forces in business, higher education, social work, politics, government, and the arts, sometimes setting records of excellence unmatched by their married peers. The association by some of them with *your* church might even lend a little "panache." Families must be made to understand that many of these individuals can serve as excellent role models for their own children, regardless of marital status.

15. DRAW UPON THE UNIQUE TALENTS OF SINGLE MEMBERS.

The single church member is apt to be less encumbered with family business and therefore more available for volunteer work. If he or she is not already involved in some capacity, perhaps it's because no one thought to ask him or her. But don't ask a lawyer to serve on your fund-raising staff; an attorney could be much more useful as a consultant on church legal matters. Similarly, an artist or a writer would probably be flattered to be asked to lend his or her creative talents to the production of some worthwhile project.

16. REQUIRE THE EASY ACCESSIBILITY OF PASTORS ON A CASUAL BASIS.

One of the most common phrases used by people in beginning a conversation with a pastor is "I know you're busy, but . . ."

Another is "I hate to bother you, but . . ." Somewhere along the line, people have got the idea that it is better to leave the pastor to "important" work than to occupy his or her already overburdened mind with such a trivial matter as the question, suggestion, or problem on their minds.

Pastors have an obligation to dispel that attitude. What more pressing business could there possibly be than the concerns and questions of people? Pastors ought to be the *most* available people around; yet on Sunday morning when the entire congregation is gathering for worship, the average pastor is virtually inaccessible. He's reviewing his sermon, checking the lights, adjusting his stole, combing his hair, and gargling. The one occasion on which he is most visible to all is when he is inaccessible on an individual basis.

Casual availability doesn't "just casually" happen, however. Wise pastors plan a coffee hour on Sunday morning following the service and do their best to let the congregation know they are readily available during the rest of the week.

17. PROMOTE A SINCERE AND SERIOUS ECUMENICAL APPROACH TO WORSHIP.

It's extremely important to recognize the value of a sincere ecumenical approach in which people of all faiths are welcomed and in fact even celebrated. People do intermarry, and when there is no great conflict between their denominations, they are apt to select the church in which they can *both* feel welcome.

Moreover, it's in the best interest of one's own congregation to focus upon the unity of faith which all have in common rather than on differences, alleged weaknesses, and supposed shortcomings.

The Apostle Paul presented a call to unity that is so clear as to discourage argument:

I, the prisoner in the Lord, implore you therefore to lead a life worthy of your vocation. Bear with one another charitably, in complete selflessness, gentleness and patience. Do all you can to preserve the unity of the Spirit by the peace that binds you together. There·is one Body, one Spirit, just as you were all called into one and the same hope when you were called. There is one Lord, one faith, one baptism, and one God who is Father of us all, over all, through all and within all (Eph. 4:1–6, JB).

18. OPPOSE LEGISLATION THAT DISCRIMINATES AGAINST SINGLES.

What could be more encouraging to hard-strapped single taxpayers than to discover that the pastor has published a "model" letter in the church paper, encouraging parishioners to write their representatives in Congress to demand federal income tax equality for singles?

"The *real crime,*" says Patty Cavin, executive director of CO$T, "lies in the varied tax charts which, since 1948, have forced us as a group to file and pay up to 20 percent to 40 percent more than income-splitting couples.

"Single and double-income married taxpayers aren't just seeking lower taxes. We want to be taxed at the same rate. It's the dollar earned that counts. Marital status should make no difference when we pay Uncle Sam."[22]

19. OPPOSE SOCIAL SECURITY REGULATIONS THAT DISCOURAGE RETIRED PERSONS FROM GETTING MARRIED.

Many elderly, retired folks prefer to live out their autumn years in lonely solitude or in what their more rigid churchgoing sons

[22]Patty Cavin, CO$T Newsletter, (February 1977): 1. *For Information Regarding Tax Discrimination of Singles:* The Committee of Single Taxpayers (CO$T), Executive Secretary: Mae Rapport, 1628 21st Street N.W., Washington, D.C. 20009 (202) 387-2678. CO$T is a nationally organized committee and publishes a newsletter periodically. Letters of protest should be sent to your Representative and to Congressman Al Ullman, Chairman, Committee on Ways and Means, 1102 Longworth, Washington, D.C. 20515 (202) 225-3625.

and daughters view as a "state of sin" rather than give up Social Security benefits to which they are entitled as single adults. It's a meager allotment, rarely enough to provide more than a sedentary, substandard way of life; but existing regulations discourage unions among retirees by mandating reductions in the monthly payments of those who give up their single status.

20. DEVELOP SPECIALIZED MINISTRIES FOR SINGLES.

Specialized ministries that explore and develop avenues of reaching alienated segments of our population, such as the unmarried, are invaluable in terms of mission work. However, they also have great value as experimental programs, providing valuable insights and information to be exchanged with others who share your concerns. In every new program is the potential for an innovation that could be applied elsewhere if it proves successful—an exciting prospect!

21. DEVELOP AN AFFIRMATIVE ACTION PLAN OF YOUR OWN, TAILORED TO THE COMMUNITY AND PARISH IN WHICH YOUR CHURCH FUNCTIONS AND UTILIZING THE IDEAS AND RESOURCES FOUND AMONG YOUR OWN MEMBERS.

And once you have done so, get the word out. Print it in your church bulletin, advise neighboring churches and other denominations of your efforts, and ask for their comments and suggestions. The development of the affirmative action plan in itself is an excellent project in which to involve previously inactive singles in an atmosphere that demonstrates you mean business.

Ask yourselves, and one another, what might be likely to get singles into the church and what would turn them off. The following table emerged from my conversations with singles in the course of more than four hundred interviews. It may be a starting point for your own exploration of the subject.

What Doesn't Get Singles into the Church	What Does Get Singles into the Church
1. Folk services	1. A pastor and people who genuinely care and are concerned.
2. New liturgy forms	
3. Coffeehouses	
4. Films, activities	2. Pure gospel orientation which you can get nowhere but the Church.
5. Debates or discussions	
6. Dating service	
	3. A feeling of being accepted and belonging.
	4. Opportunity to grow in faith and knowledge of God.
	5. Opportunity to express one's personal opinions and experience open exchange.
	6. Christian fellowship.

10. Epilogue

This book has been written from the firm belief in Talmudic wisdom that "he who knows everything is a fool." These pages are not presented as the final word about singles, the church, and a subsequent symbiosis. Rather, they are a long overdue beginning at confronting an urgent concern that cuts into the heartbeat of Christian existence.

Any effort to extract theological presuppositions or moral ethics from this book is to misrepresent its purpose. Nevertheless, some readers will undoubtedly draw assumptions to support or defend their own theological and moral rationale. I hope they will be few.

A recognition of the urgency of *millions* of singles who earnestly seek honesty, belonging, and purpose is my intended message. Churches *can* discover avenues of successful ministry to single people. There is no need for our Lord to continually weep over Jerusalem.

> O Jerusalem, Jerusalem, that kills the
> prophets and stones those sent to you,
> how often did I want to gather your
> children as a bird gathers her brood under her
> wings; and you did not care (Luke 13:34, The Berkeley Version).

This book is written with optimism. I believe the church can indeed respond to the many cries, needs, and challenges of contemporary life-styles. Such optimism is rooted in grace. Grace exists! Thank God! We can find strength in his all-sufficient grace.

Appendix A:
Continuum of
Well-being of Singles

This continuum of well-being is my subjective analysis of the singles population based on six years of ministry with them.

fluctuate uncertain about themselves			successful well-adjusted	
9%	19%	30%	31%	11%
cannot cope		average		excel

Eleven percent of the forty-eight million singles excel at whatever they do and are extremely well-adjusted people. They earn over twenty-five thousand dollars a year and are very successful people.

Thirty-one percent of the forty-eight million singles are successful and well-adjusted. They are active and involved in a meaningful way with society, endeavoring to be a vital part of today's world.

Thirty percent of the forty-eight million singles are mature, normally adjusted, average individuals who have little difficulty coping with the strains and pressures of life.

Nineteen percent of the forty-eight million singles fluctuate between being normally adjusted and being uncertain and doubtful. From time to time they lack clarity and understanding about themselves and others in society.

Nine percent of the forty-eight million singles have a great deal of difficulty coping with the problems and tensions of day-to-day life. They are most likely in need of professional help.

Appendix B:
Recent Census
Reports on Singles

TABLE A. Marital Status and Living Arrangements, March 1976

Total Adult Population 18 and Over:	145,784,000
Total Singles:	48,926,000
Never married	26,171,000
Widowed	11,812,000
Divorced	7,186,000
Separated	3,757,000
Sex:	
Women	28,342,000
Men	20,584,000

Source for pages 132–141: U.S. Bureau of the Census, *Current Population Reports,* Series P-20, No. 306, "Marital Status and Living Arrangements: March 1976," U.S. Government Printing Office, Washington, D.C., 1977.

ALL MALES		SINGLE MALES
Total (population)	77,560,000	
18 and over	69,058,000	
Single (never married)	23,106,000	
18 and over	14,656,000	14,656,000

ALL MALES		SINGLE MALES
Married, wife present	47,865,000	
18 and over	47,854,000	
Married, wife absent	2,013,000	
18 and over	1,972,000	1,352,000*
Widowed	1,793,000	
18 and over	1,793,000	1,793,000
Divorced	2,783,000	
18 and over	2,783,000	2,783,000
	Total Single Males:	20,584,000

ALL FEMALES		SINGLE FEMALES
Total (population)	84,982,000	
18 and over	76,726,000	
Single (never married)	19,527,000	
18 and over	11,515,000	11,515,000
Married, husband present	47,865,000	
18 and over	47,684,000	
Married, husband absent	3,162,000	
18 and over	3,105,000	2,405,000*
Widowed	10,020,000	
18 and over	10,019,000	10,019,000
Divorced	4,408,000	
18 and over	4,403,000	4,403,000
	Total Single Females:	28,342,000

*Includes separated persons.

AGE AT FIRST MARRIAGE

During the 16 years spanning 1960 to 1976, the estimated median age at which young men and women first marry increased by about one full year (from 22.8 years to 23.8 years for men and from 20.3 to 21.3 years for women). This and other trends observed in related statistical indicators reflect a general movement among young adults away from early marriage. For example, the estimates of the quartile ages at first marriage (the ages by which one-fourth and three-fourths of those who ever marry do so) shown in table B indicate a movement in the direction of later age

TABLE B. QUARTILES OF AGE AT FIRST MARRIAGE, BY SEX: 1963 TO 1976

Quartile of age at first marriage	1976	1975	1974	1973	1972	1971	1970	1969	1968	1967	1966	1965	1964	1963
MALE[1]														
First quartile..........	20.5	20.4	20.1	20.1	20.3	20.0	20.1	20.2	20.1	20.0	20.0	20.0	20.2	20.0
Second quartile (median).	23.8	23.5	23.1	23.2	23.3	23.1	23.2	23.2	23.1	23.1	22.8	22.8	23.1	22.8
Third quartile..........	26.9	26.5	26.6	26.4	26.2	26.4	26.2	26.0	26.3	25.8	25.8	25.9	26.1	26.4
Interquartile range[2].....	6.4	6.1	6.5	6.3	5.9	6.4	6.1	5.8	6.2	5.8	5.8	5.9	5.9	6.4
FEMALE														
First quartile..........	19.1	19.0	18.9	18.9	19.0	19.0	18.9	18.9	18.9	18.8	18.7	18.7	18.7	18.6
Second quartile (median).	21.3	21.1	21.1	21.0	20.9	20.9	20.8	20.8	20.8	20.6	20.5	20.6	20.5	20.5
Third quartile..........	24.9	24.4	24.3	24.0	23.4	23.5	23.3	23.2	23.3	22.8	22.8	22.7	22.4	22.5
Interquartile range[2].....	5.8	5.4	5.4	5.1	4.4	4.5	4.4	4.3	4.4	4.0	4.1	4.0	3.7	3.9

[1]Based on Current Population Survey data supplemented by data from the Department of Defense on marital status by age for men in the Armed Forces.
[2]Difference between first and third quartiles.

at first marriage. The central range of years during which most first marriages occur (interquartile range) is somewhat larger for men (6.4 years in 1976) than for women (5.8 years in 1976). However, in recent years this interval has broadened more for women than for men. This widening may be attributable, in part, to the increasing proportion of women who exercise options to advance their education and to gain employment prior to marriage.

Additional evidence of the changing behavior of men and women relative to first marriage is shown in table C. The proportion of the adult population under 35 years old who had never married increased between 1960 and 1976, while the proportion never married among persons 35 and over declined. Some of the increase in the percent single among the younger group is simply a function of changes in the age distribution resulting from the entry into adult ages of members of the large birth cohorts born during the high fertility years extending from the late 1940's through the early 1960's. Nevertheless, a closer inspection of the figures, particularly those for the age groups in which most first marriages take place, indicates a trend towards longer periods of singleness among young adults than in the past. The percent single for men 20 to 24 years old rose from 53 percent in 1960 to 62 percent in 1976 and from 28 percent to 43 percent during the same period for 20- to 24-year-old women. Furthermore, since 1970 the percent single among 25- to 29-year-old men and women has increased, perhaps indicating that not only has later marriage gained general acceptance but also that a higher proportion of adults will never marry during their lifetime.

DIVORCE RATIO

Another major development in recent years regarding marriage statistics has been a dramatic increase in the incidence of divorce. The National Center for Health Statistics has estimated that the divorce rate more than doubled in the last dozen years, from 2.3 per 1,000 population in 1963 to 4.8 in 1975. In March 1976 there

TABLE C. PERCENT SINGLE (NEVER MARRIED), BY AGE AND SEX: 1976, 1970, AND 1960

Age	Male					Female				
	1976	1970	1960	Change, 1970 to 1976[1]	Change, 1960 to 1970[1]	1976	1970	1960	Change, 1970 to 1976[1]	Change, 1960 to 1970[1]
Total, 14 years and over...	29.8	28.1	25.0	1.7	3.1	23.0	22.1	19.0	0.9	3.1
Under 35 years..........	56.2	54.8	50.7	1.4	4.1	45.3	44.4	37.6	0.9	6.8
35 years and over......	5.8	7.3	7.8	-1.5	-0.5	5.0	6.1	7.2	-1.1	-1.1
14 to 17 years........	99.4	99.4	99.0	-	0.4	97.0	97.3	94.6	-0.3	2.7
18 years..............	95.6	95.1	94.6	0.5	0.5	84.0	82.0	75.6	2.0	6.4
19 years..............	87.9	89.9	87.1	-2.0	2.8	72.1	68.8	59.7	3.3	9.1
20 to 24 years........	62.1	54.7	53.1	7.4	1.6	42.6	35.8	28.4	6.8	7.4
20 years..............	80.9	78.3	75.8	2.6	2.5	60.9	56.9	46.0	4.0	10.9
21 years..............	72.7	66.2	63.4	6.5	2.8	51.2	43.9	34.6	7.3	9.3
22 years..............	61.6	52.3	51.6	9.3	0.7	41.4	33.5	25.6	7.9	7.9
23 years..............	52.2	42.1	40.5	10.1	1.6	31.2	22.4	19.4	8.8	3.0
24 years..............	39.8	33.2	33.4	6.6	-0.2	26.4	17.9	15.7	8.5	2.2
25 to 29 years........	24.9	19.1	20.8	5.8	-1.7	14.8	10.5	10.5	4.3	-
25 years..............	32.1	26.6	27.9	5.5	-1.3	22.7	14.0	13.1	8.7	0.9
26 years..............	30.6	20.9	23.5	9.7	-2.6	17.4	12.2	11.4	5.2	0.8
27 years..............	23.6	16.5	19.8	7.1	-3.3	13.4	9.1	10.2	4.3	-1.1
28 years..............	22.4	17.0	17.5	5.4	-0.5	10.9	9.2	9.2	2.0	-0.3
29 years.............	16.7	13.8	16.0	2.9	-2.2	10.1	8.0	8.7	2.1	-0.7
30 to 34 years.......	12.3	9.4	11.9	2.9	-2.5	7.0	6.2	6.9	0.8	-0.7
35 to 39 years.......	7.9	7.2	8.8	0.7	-1.6	5.2	5.4	6.1	-0.2	-0.7
40 to 44 years.......	6.6	6.3	7.3	0.3	-1.0	4.2	4.9	6.1	-0.7	-1.2
45 to 54 years.......	5.6	7.5	7.4	-1.9	0.1	4.4	4.6	7.0	-0.5	-2.1
55 to 64 years.......	5.6	7.8	8.0	-2.2	-0.2	4.9	6.8	8.0	-1.9	-1.2
65 years and over....	4.4	7.5	7.7	-3.1	-0.2	5.9	7.7	8.5	-1.8	-0.8

- Represents zero

[1]Differences shown were derived by using rounded percentages.

Source of 1960 data: 1960 Census of Population, Volume I, "Detailed Characteristics," U.S. Summary, table 176.

were 2.8 million men and 4.4 million women who were reported as currently divorced (and who had not remarried) at the time of the survey. Table D shows that there were 75 divorced persons per every 1,000 persons who were partners in an intact marriage in 1976, twice as high as the corresponding ratio (35) for 1960. Moreover, this ratio has risen more in the last 6 years than during the entire 1960-to-1970 decade.

MARITAL STATUS OF PRIMARY INDIVIDUALS

In recent years the rapid growth in the number of households maintained by primary individuals (persons who either live alone or with persons not related to them) appears to be associated with observed changes in marital status. Primary individual households have increased by about 40 percent since 1970, while the total number of households increased by only 15 percent. As shown in table E, male primary individuals increased by nearly 2.5 million and female primary individuals by 2.4 million between 1970 and 1976. For men, these increases have been largely concentrated among divorced and single persons (80 percent of the total increase), whereas for women, the increase among divorced and single was about the same as that for widowed and married, spouse absent. For the youngest age group shown (under 35 years), the largest numerical increases were recorded for never-married men and women, whereas in the middle age range (35 to 64 years) the largest increases were for divorced men and women. The data for primary individuals 65 years old and over indicate that "widowed" has been and continues to be the predominant marital status for this age group.

UNRELATED ADULTS SHARING TWO-PERSON HOUSEHOLDS

As indicated above, the number of households containing primary individuals has increased by about 40 percent since 1970.

TABLE D. Number of Divorced Persons Per 1,000 Married Persons by Age, Race, and Sex: March 1976, 1970, 1965, and 1960

Sex and year	Total	Race		Age	
		White	Black and other races	Under 45 years	45 years and over
BOTH SEXES					
1976............	75	69	136	82	68
1970............	47	44	79	44	51
1965............	41	39	70	36	48
1960............	35	33	63	30	42
MALE					
1976............	58	54	103	63	53
1970............	35	32	61	31	38
1965............	34	32	56	28	40
1960............	28	27	37	22	35
FEMALE					
1976............	92	85	168	98	85
1970............	60	56	98	55	67
1965............	49	46	85	44	57
1960............	42	38	89	37	51

Note: See table A-6 in the Appendix for numerators and denominators of the ratios.

TABLE E. Primary Individuals by Marital Status, Sex, and Age: 1976 and 1970

(Numbers in thousands)

Age and marital status	1976		1970		Increase, 1970 to 1976	
	Male	Female	Male	Female	Male	Female
Total, all ages........	6,548	10,263	4,062	7,883	2,486	2,380
Married, spouse absent....	953	651	545	516	408	135
Widowed................	1,095	5,920	996	4,915	99	1,005
Divorced...............	1,530	1,290	756	844	774	446
Single.................	2,969	2,402	1,765	1,608	1,204	794
Under 35 years........	2,799	1,800	1,093	857	1,706	943
Married, spouse absent....	333	170	119	117	214	53
Widowed................	6	24	6	3	–	21
Divorced...............	432	252	125	95	307	157
Single.................	2,028	1,353	843	643	1,185	710
35 to 64 years........	2,350	3,210	1,730	2,971	620	239
Married, spouse absent....	456	335	319	307	137	28
Widowed................	262	1,467	240	1,476	22	–9
Divorced...............	904	782	507	598	397	184
Single.................	729	629	664	590	65	39
65 years and over.....	1,398	5,254	1,238	4,057	160	1,197
Married, spouse absent....	164	146	108	92	56	54
Widowed................	827	4,431	749	3,436	78	995
Divorced...............	195	258	124	152	71	106
Single.................	213	420	258	376	–45	44

- Represents zero.

During the same period the number of primary individuals who shared their living quarters with a person of the opposite sex approximately doubled (table F).

In 1976, 1.3 million persons lived in the 660,000 two-person households in which the household head shared the living quarters with an unrelated adult of the opposite sex. Seven of every 10 of these households had a male primary individual reported as the head, representing about one-half of all two-person households headed by a male primary individual. Thirty-five percent of all female primary individuals in two-person households lived with a person of the opposite sex in 1976. Seventy-two percent of the male primary individuals and 48 percent of the female primary individuals who lived with a person of the opposite sex were under 45 years old. Data in table 6 of this report show that similar proportions of men and women, about 48 percent of the men and 43 percent of the women, who headed households containing one other unrelated member of the opposite sex were reported as having never been married.

Although the increase in this type of living arrangement is notable and relevant to the study of household and family formation, caution should be exercised in interpreting the magnitude of the statistics. In order to maintain a proper perspective, it should be noted that among primary individuals in 1976, 89 percent lived alone, 9 percent lived in two-person households, and the remaining primary individuals lived in three-or-more-person households. Thus, in a general sense, unrelated adults of the opposite sex sharing living quarters as a household represent only about 4 percent of all primary individuals and only about 1 percent of all household heads. Moreover, data users who make inferences about the nature of the relationships between unrelated adults of the opposite sex who share the same living quarters should be made aware that the data on this subject are aggregates which are distributed over a spectrum of categories including partners, resident employees, and roomers.

TABLE F. Two-Person Primary Individual Households, by Age and Sex of Household Members: 1976 and 1970

(Numbers in thousands)

Sex and age of household head (primary individuals)	1976			1970[1]			Ratio (sharing): 1976/1970
	Primary individuals in 2-person households	Sharing with unrelated person of opposite sex		Primary individuals in 2-person households	Sharing with unrelated person of opposite sex		
		Number	Percent		Number	Percent	
Total..............	1,479	660	44.6	991	327	33.0	2.0
Male................	901	460	51.1	488	174	35.7	2.6
Under 25 years.......	298	108	36.2	144	21	14.6	5.1
25 to 44 years.......	425	222	52.2	163	43	26.4	5.2
45 to 64 years.......	127	85	66.9	104	59	56.7	1.4
65 years and over....	51	45	88.2	77	51	66.2	0.9
Female.............	578	200	34.6	504	153	30.4	1.3
Under 25 years.......	199	47	23.6	126	8	6.3	5.9
25 to 44 years.......	155	48	31.0	94	17	18.1	2.8
45 to 64 years.......	123	68	55.3	127	64	50.4	1.1
65 years and over....	101	38	37.6	157	64	40.8	0.6

[1] 1970 Census of Population--PC(2)-4B, Persons by Family Characteristics.

Appendix C: Profile of America's Singles

Among those 18 and over—

Number

39,875,000 or almost 30% of the adult population including:

22,865,000 who never married
11,775,000 widows and widowers
5,235,000 divorced people

Sex

Nearly 60 percent are females.

23,254,000 women
16,621,000 men

Age

Almost half are under 30.

18 to 29:	18,224,000 or 46%
30 to 44:	4,651,000 or 12%
45 to 64:	7,665,000 or 19%
65 and older:	9,335,000 or 23%

EDUCATION

A shade more than married people

	Median Years of School Completed	
	Single	Married
Males, 25 to 34 years old	12.7	12.6
Females, 25 to 34 years old	12.6	12.5

JOBS

Singles hold more of the lower-paying jobs.

	Proportion of Each Group Holding Jobs	
	Single	All Employed
Clerical workers	21.6%	17.2%
Service workers	18.1%	13.2%
Laborers	9.9%	5.1%
Farmers, farm laborers	3.9%	3.6%
Sales workers	6.3%	6.4%
Factory workers	15.9%	16.9%
Craftsmen	7.9%	13.4%
Professional, technical workers	12.3%	14.0%
Managers, administrators	4.1%	10.2%

INCOMES

Rising, but still behind those of married people.

	Average Income for Full-Time, Year-Round Workers	
	1967	1973
Single person	$5,900	$ 9,300
Married person	$7,700	$11,900

Reprinted from *U. S. News & World Report,* October 7, 1974, p. 55. Copyright 1974 U. S. News & World Report, Inc.